Where You Are & How To Get There

A Guide to Rediscovering a Life-Story Worth Living

Where You Are & How To Get There: A Guide To Rediscovering A Life-Story Worth Living

Copyright © 2022 by Nolan Recker. All rights reserved.

ISBN: 9780578288543

Unless otherwise noted, all Scripture quotations are taken from the Holman Christian Standard Bible®, Copyright © 1999, 2000, 2002, 2003, 2009 by Holman Bible Publishers. Used by permission. Holman Christian Standard Bible®, HCSB®, and Holman CSB® are federally registered trademarks of Holman Bible Publishers.

*To Emma, Zeke, and Cass,
you all inspire me to love like Jesus more,
everyday.*

*So many people to thank in this,
because what I wrote here is the
culmination of more than
ten years of ministry and life experience,
And the learning never stops.*

*I have learned something from everyone
I have had the pleasure of engaging with.*

Thank you.

What's Inside:

———··●··———

But First, A Story 11		
Questions 15		
Somewhere, Someone, Or Something 23		An Ancient Perspective
Ayeka 39		
	Decoder Key 51	
	Personality 61	
Unoriginal Practical Insight	**Pathway** 75	
	People 91	
	Purpose 101	
(W)Here You Are & How To Get (T)Here 117		This chapter has the same title as the book. :D
An Invitation	**The Process** 127	
	Rhythm & Rest 137	
Parting Thoughts: 161		Every ending is a new beginning...

5

Foreword

———··●··———

I'll forever associate Nolan with biscuits and gravy.

After starting my journey with Jesus at age 17, I ran into Nolan. He liked pizza as much as I did, rocked out to 2000s punk rock like I did, and got lost easily in conversations about big ideas like I did.

As I began to wander my way through college about an hour from where Nolan was finishing his wandering, he told me about the best biscuits and gravy he had yet found. I was in.

We met halfway every few weeks on Saturday mornings and talked about everything you could think of. I may have showed up for the biscuits and gravy, but I stayed for Nolan's curious, relatable, humble, and wise way of wandering through life.

Nolan taught me how to ask better questions. At the time, this relentless curiosity was still a latent program in my internal wiring just dying to be set free. He was optimistic, but refused to settle. His favorite part of learning was how it unlocked the next round of questions that were previously hiding under the surface.

But don't for one moment think that Nolan is just a wandering intellectual with his head in the clouds. He didn't teach me how to ask MORE questions. He taught me how to BETTER questions.

Questions are the force that drive us forward. The magic of wonder propels us into uncharted territories and invites us into the possibilities of tomorrow.

But as lovely as that sounds on paper… the *right* questions are not the most warmly welcomed.

The right questions threaten the status quo that keeps us feeling safe (even when we're not).

The right questions steal our comfort and force us into ambiguity and tension that keeps us up at night.

But the right questions also protect us from years of aimlessness and lives of regret.

When Nolan told me about the premise of this book, I was shocked at its simplicity. Something I would normally use entire conversations to get across as I sat with someone in distress or need, God had conveniently packaged in the very first question in the story of humankind.

Where are you?

The first question also happened to be the right question, and Nolan brings a compelling mixture of beauty and practicality to its potency for us all right now.

Simply put: if you can't answer this first question, there's no point in asking any others. God asked it first for a reason.

Wade into the discomfort, tension, and ambiguity - and know that grace, clarity, and purpose await you on the other side.

Tommy Carreras,
co-founder of Done with Stuck

But First, A Story

——— ··●·· ———

There is an ancient story of a man with two sons.

One day, the younger of the two sons went to the father and demanded the father immediately distribute his future allotted portion of the estate to him before his father's passing. According to the region's custom and tradition, the estate is supposed to be divided between the two sons upon the father's passing. Normally, two-thirds of the portion would go to the oldest son and the final third to the younger. Without any further interaction, the father divided the estate and gave a third to the younger son.

Within the week, the younger son gathered up all of his belongings and set out on a long journey far from home. While away from home, he lavishly spent his money without defined intentionality. After he had spent all that was given to him, he became scattered in all directions, which led to a mindset of hopelessness and purposelessness. To add insult to injury, a catastrophic famine struck and crippled the economy. Without money, meaningful relationships, or gainful employment, the son found someone who could offer him a job, as he hoped to survive by feeding their pigs. However, he was neglected and became so hungry that he longed for the same slop eaten by the pigs.

One day, he came to his senses and thought, "Even in my father's house with all of those servants, they have an abundance of bread, while I sit here starving. It would be better to return as a servant than to endure what I am experiencing here." Having awoken to his reality and what he had thrown away, he said, "I will go to my father, and I will say to him, 'Father I have forgotten you. I don't know what it means to be a son. I miss home and my place in your family. I am no longer worthy to be called "son." Please let me follow after you as a servant.'"

As he returned toward home from the far off land, word was brought to the father, "Your son is journeying toward home." The father thought, "My son remembers where he first began!" Perceiving his son had not fully understood a father's love, the father could not wait for him to arrive and instead ran to see his son. Having won the race and seeing that his son needed to be lifted up, the father pulled his son toward his heart, hugged him, and kissed his head.

With labored breath, the son began his pitch, "Father I have forgotten you. I don't know what it means to be a son. I miss home and my place in your family. I am no longer worthy to be called your…"

Before he could finish the sentence, the father interrupted him by calling some of the other servants, "My son is home! He needs clothes! Please bring out my best robe, cover him, return his signet ring, and put sandals on his feet. I am ecstatic for his return! This is cause for celebration. Bring out our best calf, it is time for a feast! My son was dead and far off, but has come back to where he belongs, alive and found!"

While the festivities ramped up, the older son finished up his daily work in the field. As he neared the house, he heard the music and saw the dancing. Confused by the unexpected partying, the son found one of the younglings and asked, "What's with all of the excitement?"

The youngling responded, "Your brother has returned home. Your father was so delighted his son is safe and well, and had to celebrate!"

Only able to think of himself, the older brother refused to enter the house.

The father perceived the oldest son had not fully understood a father's love, so he went after him and encouraged him. Instead of listening to his father and embrace his brother's return, the older son sought justice, heaping accusations toward his brother. Self-justified by his own way of living, the older brother forgot what it meant to receive his father's love. Without restraint, the older brother chastised his father for never throwing a party for all of the hard work he had done. He said, "Year after year I served you, never was I cross with you, and how many times have you shown your gratitude with a party?"

His son could not see how much of a blessing it was to always be in the father's house. Truth is, when a son who had gone astray, change his mind to leave it all behind and return home; there is no better feeling in this world or the next. "Son, you have always been there for me and all I have is yours. You are loved and blessed in this. For your brother, he was dead and removed far from this truth, but now he has awoken to who he is, open to receiving my love and affection, alive again, and found where he should be."

Questions

At first pass, do you find yourself identifying with any of the characters of this story?

This story of the man with two sons was first recorded almost 2,000 years ago. This kind of story is called a parable.

What I mean is, a parable could be fiction or non-fiction, the point isn't in the details, but in the message. Based on who tells the parable and those who listen when it is told influence how the message of the parable is interpreted.

In literature and oral traditions, parables are meant to teach something and could be compared to fables. The key difference is that parables mostly involve people, while fables tend to feature other things, animals, or mythic creatures.

Do you have a favorite book or movie?

What is it?

Who is the character you identify with the most?

Why?

If you're anything like me, you will find there are people, places, songs, movies, clothing, or even food that we appreciate more than others might. Whenever I am around those people, visit those places, listen to those songs, witness the scenes, wear my favorite jeans, or savor that first bite, something inside of me says "YES."

Have you ever experienced a sensation or thought like that?

* * *

Admittedly, I think about such things.

I dwell on them.

I will sit in a moment and take it in.

Think beyond the surface of whatever is happening and ponder on how it's all connected.

It started when I was an innocent toddler, but for the longest time, I would ask the *why* questions. Eventually, I grew up and my *why's* became more specific:

Why am I here?

Why do I like these things?

Why don't I like other things?

Why do bad things happen to me?

Why do I do bad things?

Why could I eat pizza for every meal, but others don't?

Why don't I eat pizza for every meal?

Inevitably, asking *why* leads to other questions like *what*:

What is the purpose to all of this?

What am I supposed to be doing?

What would I call a tiger mixed with a lion?

Or in the case of the younger son from the parable, "What if I could get my share of the inheritance now?"

Questions like these and many others are one of the ways we do our best to make sense of the world we live in. Oftentimes, the experiences we find ourselves in helps us to become even better.

Find ourselves.

On a daily basis, I ask a lot of questions. Just like me, you may be somewhat inquisitive or not, but there's an unrecorded question found in that ancient parable that I think all of us must have asked of ourselves at some point in our lives…

Who am I?

You may have questions like;

Who do I want to be?

Who is the person I am becoming?

Or my favorite, "Who am I, *really*?"

To me, asking "Who am I?" and "Who am I, *really*?" is a lot like asking your friend about the person they keep flirting with "Do you like them?" or "Do you like, like them?"

I have heard it said we start thinking and asking the question "Who am I?" around the time we start walking. Obviously, we aren't articulating this question consciously. I am a father of two and I don't remember either of my boys asking around eighteen months old, "Dad, who am I?"

I hear girls develop quicker than boys, so maybe the readers with daughters have experienced such a phenomenon.

At each life transition, we are both not actively thinking about and sometimes thinking about asking the question, "Who am I?"

When we were toddlers and had our first experience of independence, we communicated as best we can whenever we wanted to be free and move about a space. What this means is that we are recognizing a sense of separation between ourselves and our caregivers.

Each new "first" in our lives impacts and influences how and what we think about ourselves.

And if you're human, the older and more aware you become, the more you will not only think about "Who am I?" but will battle against "Who do other people think that I am?"

The way we wrestle with certain questions will impact and influence the people we surround ourselves with, the characters/people we identify with in stories, the clothes we wear, the dreams we dream, the art we consume, the food we eat, and even the belief systems we form to give us a sense of purpose & meaning.

I love the parable of the man with two sons because it touches on so many ideas (in no particular order):

family, identity, self-awareness, money, desire, discontent, best intentions, immaturity, grace, justification, justice, love, celebration, redemption, reconciliation, parenting, siblings, historical & cultural insight, traditions, rituals, significance, forgiveness, religion, spirituality, purpose, meaning, perspective, and perception.

I bet you could add more words to that list.

Maybe you can take a couple more minutes to go back and read the parable again.

Before we can answer the question "Who am I?" we need to look at some other frequently asked questions in order to find the right one.

* * *

Have you ever been in a situation where you asked the question

"How did I get here?"

There have been a few times when I drove to some place, zoned out while driving, arrived at my destination and wondered, "I don't remember some of my trip." One time, I got lost in a corn maze. I stared at my phone, checking fantasy football while only taking right turns inside the maze. Before I knew it, I doubled back twice and had no clue on where to go. Then it began to rain, and it got really muddy. I called the staff to send a maze runner to find me.

Or maybe you have worked on a project with others and someone asked, "Where are we with the T.P.S. report?"

That kind of question is more mechanical or technical than a question about the essence or being of a thing. No one asks what the T.P.S. report thinks about itself.

I am not talking about those kinds of "How did I get here?" moments.

I am talking about being in a relationship with a significant other where it started off great, but along the way, things changed. Suddenly, you two grew distant. Then, you wonder,

"How did we get here?"

Maybe you have felt stuck in a job. Instead of following after the dreams of your youth, "reality" crept in and you settled for something less than what you hoped would happen.

Maybe you've been overwhelmed by bills, the amount of debt you owe, and asked the *how did I get here* question…

I mean those types of situations where there is a literal explanation to the "how" certain things went certain ways, certain decisions were made, and how those things culminated in an unexpected season of life.

When we ask the question "how," most of the time we aren't asking for an explanation.

Oftentimes, we are really asking "Why?" Though this question is more about wanting to know or understand something, maybe seeking some sort of explanation, as if we need someone or something to blame.

This phenomenon is so commonplace we think knowing the reason for something will make it better or easier to understand and accept.

Why did that person drink, drive, and kill my daughter?

Why didn't God save my marriage?

Why did the bank lend me that money?

Why didn't the President pass a better tax bill like they promised?

These questions seem right whenever we ask them.

How often does satisfaction come from the answers to these questions? If something didn't work out the way we wanted it to, asking "why" is part of the process, but we often get distracted by the pain or disappointment.

We cope.

We deny the pain and move on with our lives.

Eventually, we find ourselves asking the same questions over and over, as though we are only taking right turns in a corn maze. Before we know it, we are the furthest point away from where we started and the rain begins to pour.

Because I believe our three big questions stem from the same root issue, hence, this book is an attempt to bring some form of clarity many of us could use.

Instead of chasing after the next fad program, unhealthy addiction, mid-life crisis purchase, or a sabotaged sense of our purpose, let's learn to find a new rhythm of discovering our starting point.

When our selfish ambition seeks an early stake in our Father's inheritance, we isolate ourselves from loved ones, looking for fulfillment, only to realize we miss home…

When our lives are not in a place we thought would be, we tend to ask "Where do you see yourself in five years?"

When we are transitioning from one life stage to another without much vision for the future…

When you feel like you have been floating through life, as if life is happening to you and you are not happening to life…

These questions, these life situations, all influence each other.

There is a better question to ask.

And it all begins with YOU.

Somewhere, Someone, Or Something

There's a lot to identify with in the parable about the man with two sons. And we will get into it throughout this book. Specifically, how all of us in some way are like the younger son. We have all experienced that place where we ask the questions or make these resolutions,

"How did I get here?"

"Why did this happen?"

"I need to change something."

There is another story I want to share that will help us understand the disconnect we all have felt within ourselves at some point. This story is written in the form of a poem.

It can be found in ancient Jewish literature and it talks about the things of earth, time and space. It introduces the idea of a god-being and how humankind is a lot like this god. It even goes so far as to explain how each person has meaning and a unique purpose.

There is much to discover in the poem.

There are epic beginnings and prophesied endings. A cosmic battle of dark versus light, and in there are intricate details, beautiful imagery, and world-building. We can read about the mythic explanation of the universe's arch bent toward eternal love and justice.

You would also find the disruption of relationships and why your significant other can never decide on what they want to eat. They tell you to make a choice, and when you do, you get it wrong. Then they say they're not picky and are up for whatever, so you submit another idea and that too gets denied. All of the sudden you find yourself debating about how many times you can wear a pair of jeans before considering them dirty and in need of a wash.

Okay, maybe not all of that is in there, but you have been there, right? Not everything in our relationships is rainbows, candy, and puppies.

This ancient poem outlines the fractured sense of our human condition and the hyperbolic threat of death.

It is also in this poem that we find the first question ever attributed to a god-being: Yahweh, God, or Allah—according to the three primary monotheistic faiths, Judaism, Christianity, and Islam.

The way people have looked at or tried to understand this god-being—especially within the three major world religions—has splintered time after time. The way people treated other people from different religious backgrounds is something many people are familiar with. Never mind how people within specific religions can unfairly treat each other, for the negative effects of religion often stick with us longer than the supposed benefits.

There is a truth to everything, though.

Meaning, a common truth exists.

Is God real? This is not the book to answer that question. However, this is the book to discuss our life's response to the idea God is real.

The makeup of our world on a microscopic or cellular level speaks to this. If you have heard of atoms, protons, neutrons, or electrons. If you can remember anything from the periodic table of elements, things like oxygen and hydrogen. The way things interact with each other have a pre-determined outcome.

For example, scientists have been able to determine that the earth is actually tilted—not straight up and down—at an angle of 23.5 degrees. If it were to be moved more than a degree in either direction, life on this planet would be unrecognizable.

These kinds of truths are known as "laws." They describe the ways things work and how what we know and experience would be drastically different if any of these "laws" were to change. In a way, these truths are common for everyone.

Another example would be gravity. Have you ever experienced a fall or an imbalance and crash to the earth? You encountered gravity and it affects everyone.

Like these physical truths, there are probably truths that are common amongst people in a less obvious way.

Many people in history claimed to possess this common truth.

It even happens today.

This claim of knowing the whole truth and nothing but the truth is peddled in many ways and expressed by all sorts of people. In a way, this book could be interpreted in that way. In exploring stories to help us make sense of a commonality amongst all of us, we flirt with the notion that the truths found within are actually common for all people.

I don't claim to know the whole truth, but I believe I at least found the door.

Regarding religious, scientific, political, sociological, economical, or philosophical differences, this is not the space where I attempt to directly reconcile the similarities and differences among these areas of thought.

In the pursuit of a commonality for all people, I believe in a singular explanation for the existence of all things. Meaning all of what we think must stem from a

"somewhere," a

"someone," or a

"something."

In a way, we all live in a way where we try to make sense of our experiences. We are very good at making common connections. We like people that like the same things as us. We like to eat food we know we like. We all have our habits, rituals, and traditions, which is part of being human. Even the most unorganized people in our lives still have a system of how they keep things "in order."

In quantum physics, there are a number of researchers searching to find a unifying theory of existence or a singularity from which all of life can be understood.

It makes sense, doesn't it?

We experience and make sense of our lives through the lens of starting points and ending points.

For some, they prefer the explanation of our origin backstory being more chaotic.

It's all a crazy random happenstance!

It might be.

That is part of what makes this life so exciting. No matter the origin, if you're alive, you have the chance to make this life into any number of things. Where, when, and to whom you were born has its effect. Overall, more so than any other time in human history, at least here in America and other developed countries, people are able to almost do anything they set their heart to doing or accomplishing.

In the early pages of the ancient Jewish poem is the mythic legend of a god-being who goes to work creating things.

Beginning with nothing but a darkened canvas, this creator-god-being turned on the lights and made things. From a formless nothing into formed things; from sky and water to land and air, and from animals, fish, and birds to fill those spaces. There are celestial patterns to mark the created order of time. The poem concludes the narrative of creative events with the manifestation or incarnation of the creator-god-being's essence and being into a tangible form and likeness.

Going from a formless nothing to us would be more like creating with clay before there was clay or even the idea of it.

It's like having the idea for something, and not being sure of how to make it happen. But in order to make it happen, you have to make something else. And because that thing doesn't yet exist, you then create something else in order to create that one thing you pictured.

If you have ever heard of the phrase "reverse-engineering," it means to begin your work with the end in mind. You visualize what it is you are aiming to accomplish or create and then work backwards to determine what your first next step is. The amount of steps in between your first step and the final step-- the finished product-- could sometimes be measured to the nth degree.

As a kid, I enjoyed building with LEGOS. They are toy blocks that connect with each other to form shapes and patterns. They are different from wood blocks that easily stack and knock over. They have notches that latch with other pieces. What the creators do for a design is a picture of the final product and then give you a direction book showing you steps on how to build it.

I have two kids and they both love building with LEGOS. They enjoy when I play with them because I will build elaborate things without following any instructions.

"How did you build that, Dad?"

They like following instructions to build the final design they see on the box. Thinking of something that doesn't exist yet, building it, and then playing with it is the closest we can understand creating something out of nothing.

This is what the three major world religions believe. At the center of everything lies a being that made all things.

The smallest known particle cannot be seen with just our eyes. We need powerful electron microscopes to see the atoms that make up our existence. Atoms are in everything. The word "atom" means indivisible.

Scientists, in their pursuit to discover the center of everything, have split the atom to see what is inside. Like a child to a piñata, so scientists have done to the atom. Unfortunately, there's no candy inside an atom, but neither were the answers scientists were hoping for. Atoms are made up of those protons, neutrons, and electrons. Beyond what we know, there's a lot to discover there, and an explanation on how the world got here still eludes us all.

Yet, here we are.

Humans.

Talking about things called atoms.

Wondering why they are still reading this book and not streaming their favorite show.

I have this audacious idea that we are the unifying theory to everything.

That's right.

Humans.

Are.

The.

Answer.

YOU are the—

Okay.

Let me back up.

Let's get back to the ancient poem about the beginning of all things.

The poem says that basically, humans are like a self-portrait of the creator-god-being. We are more than just the conglomeration of a mom and dad; our origin story goes back further, to a God whom created everything. If this is true, then humans are—in a more fancy way of saying—

a finite image of an infinite presence and effect.

Clears up all confusion, yeah?

According to legend, the first human creature was called *man*. Mostly because the language used to write the poem had harder and softer aspects to it. In the English language, we have consonants and vowels. The writer of the poem didn't use

English. Their language is understood through masculine and feminine, harder sounds and softer sounds. If you have studied or speak the Spanish language at all, then this idea isn't new to you. It may not seem important, but it really is.

The masculine aspect of the language has led people to interpret the ancient text in specific ways. Based on your faith background—if you have one— you have probably heard of the god-being as a "He" or "Him."

So, the first "human" was a man and because man was created in the image of his creator, the creator must be some form or "him."

However, the poem tells about how the man was alone and it wasn't good for him to be alone. The creator-god-being (let's shorten it to Creator) put the man to sleep, removed a rib bone, made another human, and then had the man wake up.

The man wakes up and calls the new human "woman." The author of the poem used feminine language to describe "her."

The Creator brought out of the man, much like the Creator brought out of Himself, an image bearer.

So the poem goes that this Creator made both man and woman. Through the intimate relationship of the man and woman, other image bearers would come.

For the Creator, the masculine and feminine aspects of the being's essence and effect are represented in man and woman. The Creator saw to it that being singular wasn't right, but in terms of life and purpose saw one created man could not wholly possess what the Creator is "made of" and put it in two different expressions—man and woman.

The Creator took matter, formed it, and from His own "breath" or "spirit," He animated (brought to life) the man. Convincing arguments have been given to both justify and deny our physical forms being a representation of the Creator, as if he is in some other unseen realm appearing in human form. Whether this is true or not, it is not answered in this book. Primarily, as we get into the later chapters, it's not so much about what we look like, but moreso the way we live, work, relate, and play. Our way of living serves as a mirror, reflecting what we believe about the Creator and an understanding of our collective origin story.

The imagery in the poem shows us two things were necessary for us to become real.

One part creative eternity (something infinite like a god) and the other part created matter (something finite).

This is compounded in the symbolism of man and woman.

Two existing parts coming together in order to make a singular new person. A man by himself or a woman by herself lack the ability to create baby versions of themselves on their own.

For some reason, this Creator-God needed to have some fun and created an asexual Seahorse that produces other asexual Seahorses on their own.

Why?

No idea.

Random thought, but it's true.

* * *

Now, the poem has been read in a variety of ways. Simply, there are three primary ways to read it. Literally, allegorically, and a made-up word; nuance-ly (or dynamically).

For the sake of brevity, here is the basic break down of the three.

Literally- means that what is written is what happened. The Creator God is a real supernatural being. Beyond our exhaustive comprehension. There was literally one man, one woman, etc. Each day was literally a 24-hour period. There was a (spoiler alert) literal serpent with a literal fruit tree. Man looks like the Creator-God and Creator-God looks like man.

Allegorically- means that what was written is a lot like the ancient parable at the beginning of this book. There may or may not be a supreme supernatural being. There may or may not have been a singular man and a singular woman. The serpent could have been imagery representing the thoughts that pit us against the Creator-God. The trees are thought patterns.

Nuancely- means that the Creator-God is probably real, but in a capacity that we can only know His part, not His whole. There may have been two people to start because we know people are real, so it all had to start somewhere. The serpent, man, woman, and a piece of fruit could have been real actors. They ate that literal fruit, but the fruit adversely affected the way they viewed and related with the Creator-God, themselves, others, and the creation man was to oversee. Like the parable, the lesson from the story probably matters more than the potential literalism.

If you are from the United States, we are subject to thinking dualistically or in binary categories. We distill things, ideas, and also people into two categories.

Good & Evil

Black & White

Right & Wrong

Life & Death

Rich & Poor

Success & Failure

Ford & Chevy

Okay, maybe the last one isn't on the list, but you get the point. *Literal* and *allegorical* were the two major interpretative camps of the early faith-in-Jesus-movement. Two different schools sprang up in what is now modern day Middle East and Africa, Antioch and Alexandria. The Antioch school read the ancient texts primarily through a literal lens while the Alexandrian school read through an allegorical lens.

Allegory leans *nuance*. However you want to envision the varying levels of influence active in any given situation or interaction, it has the room for the shades of gray, all the colors on the light spectrum, or reading between the lines.

Reorienting how we view or interpret things is the necessary shift for us to have a deeper understanding of our lives.

For the man and woman in the poem, they were formed and fashioned by the Creator-God, were called "good" and given a five-fold directive:

Be fruitful.

Multiply.

Fill the earth.

Subdue it.

Rule over it.

The poem ends with clarification on what to eat. Spoiler alert: You're to be vegetarians.

Before you throw this book in the trash, bear with me.

See what I did there.

Jokes aside, let's keep going.

There is a disparity of understanding in regards to the ancient poem. Something changed in the writing and the tone from "You're to be vegetarians" to a summation of the poem.

Furthermore, the poem said the man and woman were naked and felt no shame.

The text changes from a poetic song to more of a historical record. Whatever was or wasn't in the beginning of all things took a turn in the writer's account of events. In the traditional referencing of the material, translators make a break between the poem in the writing's first and second chapter.

In the second and third chapter, we could see more details about the woman and the one non-negotiable given by the

Creator-God. The non-negotiable was "eat of every tree *except* the one in the *middle* called *knowledge of good & evil.*"

If you are familiar with the Christian and Jewish version of events, the man and the women directly violated the order to refrain from the tree in the middle. Arguably, the man and the woman were content with not eating of its "fruit" until the text revealed a fourth character—the serpent submitting a different idea for the man and woman to consider.

The serpent or in the ancient langue, "the cunning one," asked a leading question to the unsuspecting people.

Earlier, I introduced how we ask all sorts of questions. I imagine some questions are better than others.

The question by "the serpent" casted doubt in the minds of the man and woman. The doubt was one of a perceived disconnection between them and the Creator-God.

"If God can eat from this tree, why can't we?"

Upon consuming the fruit of this question, the writer wrote, "Immediately, their eyes were opened."

If you're following along with me, when it says "their eyes were opened," it wasn't literal. They weren't blind in the physical sense, but to something more intangible or invisible.

Their "seeing" was a light bulb moment, revelatory, but in an unwelcome way. The man and woman "realized" they were "naked" and each of them responded by trying to cover themselves.

Based on your understanding of this Creator-God, you may be familiar with this.

Based on the tradition of *faith* (we all have faith in something, even if it is in "nothing," however not everyone of us would identify as "religious") in which you grew up, you may have a memory of this story and the Creator-God's reaction or sentiment toward the man and woman.

Have you ever felt the tinge of guilt whenever you let someone down or they were disappointed with you?

That thought stems from this story.

When we feel that guilt, we are recognizing our wrongs in our relationship with that person.

For the man and the woman, they realized they were not the same as their Creator-God. They self-identified a sense of disconnection between themselves and their Creator.

Immediately, they began blaming others for this new unwelcomed sense of awareness. This new awareness created a domino effect of broken relationships and how to navigate them.

In love, the Creator-God sought after them with a one-word question.

Ayeka

——··●··——

"**A**yeka?" - God

This one-word question inspired this entire book.

The word is Hebraic in origin and translates to an English phrase,

"Where are you?"

Let's pick up the story from its source:

Of all the wild creatures the Eternal God had created, the serpent was the craftiest.

Serpent (to the woman): Is it true that God has forbidden you to eat fruits from the trees of the garden?

Woman: No, serpent. God said we are free to eat the fruit from the trees in the garden. We are granted access to any variety and all amounts of fruit with one exception; the fruit from the tree found in the center of the garden. God instructed us not to eat or touch the fruit of that tree or we would die.

Serpent: Die? No, you'll not die. God is playing games with you. The truth is that God knows the day you eat the fruit from that tree you will awaken something powerful in you and become like Him, possessing knowledge of both good and evil.

The woman approached the tree, eyed its fruit, and coveted its mouth-watering, wisdom-granting beauty. She plucked a fruit from the tree and ate. She then offered the fruit to her husband who was close by, and he ate as well. Suddenly, their eyes were opened to a reality previously unknown. For the first time, they sensed their vulnerability and rushed to hide their naked bodies, stitching fig leaves into crude loincloths. Then they heard the sound of the Eternal God walking in the cool misting shadows of the garden. The man and his wife took cover among the trees and hid from the Eternal God.

God (calling to the man): Where are you?

Man: When I heard the sound of You coming in the garden, I was afraid because I am naked. So I hid from You.

The exchange as read above comes from The Voice Translation Reader's Bible. Like the younger son in the parable of the man with two sons, I see something similar here in this story of the man and the woman.

I submit for your consideration, that shortsightedness, blindness, or willful ignorance of all available facts led to decisions that ended up working against the younger son, man, and the woman.

In the case of the younger son, if he had been able to see (realize) what he already possessed in his father's house, he would not have left in the first place.

For the man and the woman, had they trusted God's direction to refrain from the "fruit" of that one "tree," they would not have noticed what God had not yet revealed to them.

The legend of the man and the woman precedes the parable of the man with two sons by thousands of years. Taking into consideration the ramifications of the man and woman, it made me wonder about the younger son from the parable. I wonder about his thought life. What were the kinds of questions he asked himself? What questions did he ask and answer that eventually led to the desire to leave home?

Did the son really know where he was while living in the father's house?

Did the man and woman really know where they were while living in the Creator-God's garden?

* * *

Why the emphasis on this question "Where are you?"

For the collection of writings from where this question comes, this is the first-ever recorded question from the Creator-God.

The word 'ayeka' is collision of two words, "Where" and the Hebrew root word we translate into English, "You."

Translating ancient languages into modern ones, is in its own right—a journey. What I am trying to do is to propose borderlines on an oversimplified understanding of the word, YOU. Again, for us Western Hemisphere readers, we want distilled and simple.

"Give me the PLAIN truth! Don't wrap it up in your fancy nuancely-made-up-word-nonsense. I want to be certain about the things I think I know."

I hear you. I really do. I get it. Uncertainty can be a scary thing; being unsure what to believe is a big deal. Look at the story of the man and the woman with the half-eaten fruit. If they were certain about the Creator-God's instruction, would they have eaten the fruit?

That question doesn't matter much anymore.

As my animated friend from The Lion King movie once said, "You can't change the past! You can either run from it, or learn from it."

Let's learn some things from this.

It's all about,

YOU.

The Hebrew word behind the English word YOU is three Hebrew letters.

Aleph.

Tov.

Hey.

Using other references from the ancient Hebrew texts, we can learn and interpret what these words mean. First, you need to be reminded that this ancient Hebrew language is referred to as a dynamic language. Meaning, each letter is also a number, a word, and a picture.

The English language is not only difficult, but boring.

The Creator-God in these ancient writings is reported to be all-knowing, ever-present, and all-powerful. So this everywhere, all the time, and "knows everything" kind of deity certainly would have been privy of all the activities going on in His garden. Certainly, there would have been some prior knowledge of the visiting serpent. (Again, assuming some sort of literal interpretation of the story.)

God's first response to the man and woman is a question of the geographical reference variety, "where are you?"

As we have set up to this point, it probably was not a geographical question.

Taking all of these things into consideration, there must have been a calculation in His inquiry.

What if the question wasn't for God?

What if the question was for *us*?

The one word Hebrew question comes from the root word we translate as "YOU."

The pictures and meanings for each of the letters in the word YOU give us a different way of considering the impact of this word.

YOU are the most important thing in all of Creation. But why?

* * *

When we consider the interaction between God, the serpent, the man, and the woman, we can go a bit deeper in the interplay.

God created the man and woman in His image. Nowhere in the poem do we see the man and woman considering the created difference between themselves and their Creator-God. Meaning, they may have viewed themselves within a certain framework and unity with their Creator.

Their "eyes" focused on something beyond what the text declares. The serpent suggested to the man and woman that God got to partake in all the trees of the garden, but not them. They were to abstain from just one tree. I believe this was an accusation disguised as a suggestion.

To us, it doesn't seem like a big deal. I can have all of the other trees? Deal. I can trade one for everything else.

Except, the man and the woman doubled back on this process. The serpent questioned how the man and woman were looking at things. When asked to reconsider what God really said about the tree they were not to eat from, the woman added that she heard God say she couldn't even touch it. In the poem, God never commanded the man and woman to avoid touching the tree. The serpent told the man and woman that if they "ate" of the tree, they would become like God.

Weren't they already like God?

If they were really like God, could they not eat from the same tree?

In that moment of "eating the fruit," the man and the woman saw themselves apart from the Creator-God they once viewed themselves in unity with.

YOU in the Hebrew gives us three pictures.

Aleph - The beginning.

Tov - The end.

Hey - Breath of God.

The Creator-God was before humankind and will still be after humankind. It was His breath that gave life to humankind. For the ancients, to be both beginning and the end doesn't point to a limitation of God. Instead, it is an exaggeration of our understanding of space and time. God is beyond, above, below, and within anything we know.

This God cannot be fully known, but He can be experienced around and within ourselves.

God's declaration to a shame-filled people hiding behind some pithily plant produce pants was one of the affirmations of His vision of the man and woman.

"I am the beginning and the end, breathed into you."

If one believes God to be real in the experiential sense, then this language-imagery is an incredible reminder.

No matter where we view ourselves in relation to our proximity to God, we cannot escape the fact that the very fundamental makeup of our existence is wrapped up in Him. If I believe in God, then I am implored to believe whatever God intentionally put into humankind is the *stuff of before, the now, and the not yet.*

Awake or asleep, conscious or unconscious, we are of an eternal origin with an eternal destination in God.

One way of interpreting the Christian narrative as played out through ancient writings assimilated together into what we would call The Bible;

is the tragic hero's arch toward redemption.

There is a common thread woven throughout the collection of those writings:

the God of the Bible wants to reaffirm us of who He is *for* us and not what we think He has *against* us.

Based on your experience with church or the number of sermons you have heard, that statement may be triggering. There's a lot of decent arguments out there painting God to be a wrathful, angry, and offended Creator. This book isn't the space to counteract those perceptions and views, but there are other great books out there to read on the topic.

For the sake of this book, we are working off the premise that God has never given up hope for His creation.

By asking the question "Where are you?" He presented to all of us a way to think about our lives: "It's time to take a hard look at where we truly ARE—the person we are, what we have done with our lives, what we are doing with our time, heart, and mind—and then compare that with where we want to go."[1]

God's desire to be known and for us to be known by Him is more explicitly played out in the New Testament collections of writings found in the Bible. Here, the confusion of the Old Testament and the fragile arguments of "that God's" character are brought into greater clarity through the historical Jesus.

* * *

The reason for our dive into this ancient question is that like the other questions we inevitably ask ourselves on a daily basis, *Ayeka* is the foundational one.

When we experience the fruit of new information, what is our response?

When it came to interacting with a deity, the man and woman hid themselves.

God came along and brought a revelation and a reminder of who they really were and were created to be.

For us today, in a time and space of seemingly infinite access to information and resources unprecedented in the history of humanity, how do we respond?

Alongside the information is our appetite for consumption. It goes beyond food. The man and woman in the ancient poem responded with covering and hiding. The younger son in the parable hid by leaving his home and covered his discontent with partying and carousing.

The oldest recorded question by the Creator-God was echoed by the younger son. The younger son considered where he was, where the servants of his father's house were, and he made a decision to accept the miscalculation.

But having come to his senses, the younger son decided to go home.

This is what God invited the man and woman to do when He asked "Where are you?"

The man and woman didn't know how to respond. Simply, God was calling the man and woman back to who they really were—not just how they saw themselves.

This is what the father in the parable did. The younger son could not finish his apologetic petition to return as a slave because the father saw his boy as a son, one whom was always a part of the house, even though the son sought to be disconnected from it.

The son didn't know what he was asking for when he asked for the inheritance. The same could be said of the man and the woman; they didn't know what kind of awareness they were asking for.

In a world full of options, narratives, and destinations, without many restraints or conditions to pursue much of what you want to pursue, you may feel a tinge of "lostness." A sense you are floating through life. With so much demanding your attention and money, you may often find it hard to feel at peace.

If you don't really know where you are in relation to a lot of things, it's time to discover the way back to yourself. The you God had in His mind's eye before creating you.

Hopefully, as you take the steps to discover where you really are right now, maybe then you will be able to determine what your next step is on this adventure we call life.

Decoder Key

When the man and the woman discovered their new found sense of awareness, the way they viewed themselves, God, and the world around them changed.

If you were to read the source material in a nearby Bible, you could read in more detail what transpired after that initial interaction.

For the sake of brevity, I will list the four major areas of disruption caused by the shift in the man and woman's perspective and perception.

"Self" - They saw themselves as naked and felt shame.

"Others" - They blamed each other and the serpent for eating the fruit, neglecting personal responsibility.

"God" - They had to leave the garden.

"Creation" - The world was going to cause thorns and thistles for the man and woman.

Based on your sense of proximity to these four areas, you will be able to determine your level of self-awareness about your life and the steps you need to take toward living the life God desires for you.

There is a game I discovered in a newspaper which I really like to play. Who reads a physical paper and ink newspapers anymore? Not me, but I do like playing Cryptoquip. In our local paper, one would find the Crossword, Wordfind, and Sudoku on the same page.

The goal of Cryptoquip is to decode the jumbled letters into a one-line quip. At first glance, it is all gibberish. However, the creators give what one of the gibberish letters really represents. For example, whenever there is an "L", it could actually mean a "S." Once you start swapping out the L's with S' it gives clues to what the other letters really represent.

In order to discover the way back to ourselves, we must begin with the decoder key of sorts in hopes of gaining a better understanding of what God's original intention is for every person, specifically in relation to the four major disrupted areas.

That decoder key is the personhood of *Jesus.*

Jesus was a historical person whom near the end of His life claimed to be the Son of God. One of the writers in the New Testament of the Bible described Jesus as the exact representation of the Creator-God. The same writer explained to some people how the original intention for the way humanity was to operate is different than much of our experience. How each of us are to relate and interact within Ourself, Others, God, and Creation is revealed in Jesus the person, the Prophet, the Priest, the King, etc.

The writer calls the way of Jesus a "mystery." The further humanity got from the conversation between the man, woman, and God, the more those four major areas of disruption compounded.

Mystery, in this sense, means the way of Jesus was hidden from seeing. The way of allowing oneself to be seen by God, be loved by Him, to have a sense of belonging; and in response to this love, lay your life down for the sake of others.

2,000 years ago, humanity as a whole lost their inherent sense or understanding of what it really meant to be human. Their worldviews, myths, meanings, purpose or sense of purposelessness was distorted to the way of Jesus.

Since Jesus had been hidden by our sense of spiritual amnesia, people went on believing all sorts of things about life and God. In other words, humanity's perspective and perception were darkened. Jesus came as a light to expose the shadows in the dark.

I went to college with a guy who suffered from night blindness. One night, while driving, he stopped his car in time to avoid striking something he saw in the street. Putting the transmission in park, he opened his door and put one foot out to stand and speak with the person he was about hit, who was curled up in a ball in the middle of the road. "Hey man! You alright? You're in the middle of the road!"

The man didn't respond. My friend was concerned. "This dude is acting really weird."

After another few awkward moments, he got up the courage to walk up to the man and confronted him, not in a mean way, but to figure out why the man was in the middle of the street.

As he got closer, within a couple feet away, my friend reached out to tap the man on his shoulder, and suddenly the man began to wave like a plastic bag in a medium breeze.

The man was no man at all. "It" was a black industrial sized garbage bag. My friend felt so foolish. Not even the headlights on his car were strong enough to counteract the minimal amount of light his eyes let in. During the day, his vision was relatively normal. At night, shadows could be anything.

In the same part of the New Testament where the way of Jesus was a mystery but now revealed, it says, "But when the completion of the time came…Jesus came."

I think what the writer meant was the revelation of Jesus needed to come at just the right time. Humanity did not earn the time, but we could assume that on a certain level an appropriation of specific events and evolution of culture occurred, allowing God the opportunity—in accordance with the way Creation is set up—to send a savior in Jesus Christ.

There is an unseen order of things in the universe.

This would be a good time to acknowledge that if there is a sense of freedom or free will programmed into Creation, then it could offer up a partial explanation as to the existence of divergence from good in the forms evil. "Evil" in terms of an absence of love, service, humiliy, gentleness, and goodwill toward eachother. It would also give the basis for beings like demons and Satan.

Evil in the simplest sense means the "absence of goodness."

Paul explained in the first chapter of his letter to a church in Galatia, "Our Lord Jesus Christ gave Himself up for our sins to rescue us from this present evil age, according to the will of our God and Father…"

This is the Gospel message Christians are supposed to be telling everyone. Paul goes on to say the gospel is not based on a "human point of view." There is some other, let's say godly point of view.

The good news of this gospel is the whole Jesus thing.

In the Christian worldview, Jesus came from God and identified Himself as the Son of Man (and we, in turn, refer to Him as the Son of God. Both parts of this help people understand who they are.) This gives Jesus credibility to the physical side of our created being.

Ancient humanity, in our darkened understanding became predisposed with the physical so much so they forgot their spiritual life force. Jesus reconciled this and said, "I am a child of the earth as much as you."

Then, Jesus displayed for people what a man can accomplish when he cooperates with the source of their true identity. Jesus walked out a renewed connection with God. Up until the point of Jesus, the disconnection between God and His creation was so severe that the only solution was for God to become man in Jesus and fulfill the requirements already at work in the heavens. If this is new to you, I admit it sounds kind of ridiculous. Even more so, Jesus died, rose from the dead, and countless amounts of people were willing to die as they testified to this equally crazy claim.

Jesus wanted people to know that God was not (and never was) an "angry God." God even said in front of multiple witnesses on a couple of occasions, "This is my son [Jesus], in whom I am well pleased." Jesus came to speak for God. "I only do what I see my Father doing in heaven."

Jesus worked to take the blinders off people by healing the sick, feeding the hungry, and raising the dead. He performed signs and wonders to help people experience the Father's love they sorely misunderstood.

* * *

For the sake of clarity and portability, let's see the four areas Jesus came to repair and offer up some coordinating language:

Self - Personality

Others - People

God - Pathway

Creation - Purpose

If you haven't thought about these four areas in this way before, I hope our unpacking of these principles along with actionable next steps will demystify things for you. For us in the

West, we are used to a linear or vertical way of thinking. Step one, step two, step three, etc.

We move through school one grade and one level at a time. We climb the corporate ladder by beginning at the bottom and working upward. We build a house by laying a foundation and building upon that. We become "adults" by the age of eighteen. In many ways, we think there are certain things we are supposed to accomplish at certain "ages."

A lot of this was driven by hierarchical understandings of human development. It is influenced by the production-line efficiency of early manufacturing breakthroughs. There is an inevitable line all people must follow. At times, people diverge and create their own line and disrupt our entire way of thinking.

Our brains work well with this too. Every picture, movie, sound, food, feeling, scent, etc. Every sensation we experience is logged in our brain somewhere. If something is "new" to us, it gets its own new database to store those similar sensations. If the "new" thing is similar to some other sensation we previously experienced, it gets an imaginary string connected to all the similar aspects of that experience.

Metaphorically, our brain in our conscious awareness likes easy to sort experiences within the pre-developed databases of previously experienced situations. In this, we think in a line or put things in a box. However, our brain works more like a network of connections with strings crisscrossing all over the place. The outdated adage that women's brains are like spaghetti and men's are like waffles is not really true.

All people have similarities in the way we think and sort information. And no matter how much you think you can or cannot multitask, the truth is that none of us can multitask. We can only focus on one thing at a time and with each switch of our focus, we burn calories and mental energy.

It shouldn't surprise us if we don't feel like we are fully harmonizing our personality, pathway, purpose, and people into a fully realized understanding of life.

Have you ever felt tired at the end of the day and aren't sure why?

Have you ever felt like you needed to distance yourself from someone, but don't have an obvious reason?

Has God ever felt distant from you?

Are you working in a job that offers little on the surface in reference to joy or fulfillment?

All these questions fall into the four disrupted areas Jesus came to reorient us for a better understanding.

The path back to yourself can begin with any of the four areas, but I don't want to be legalistic about it. All four of these areas need to be harmonized to have the best starting point for answering "Where are you?"

I have found in my journey that a great place to begin is with my personality default responses. In other words, a renewed sense of how I operate in my day-to-day, situational self when faced with normal circumstances .(Personality)

From there, I want to leverage my sense of spirituality by gaining a fresh understanding of the ways I best connect with the "more of this life," "the transcendent," or the God that created me. (Pathway)

I start with those two because my relationship with God is very personal. However, I was not created to live life alone. That means my faith journey is intimately personal, but it is also profoundly communal. This leads me to the question "how I can better relate with people?" (People)

Since I am human, I am limited. Different theories abound about how many people we can really have a meaningful relationship with. Furthermore, research has discovered the importance of having meaningful friendships with others is a commonality amongst people living to the age of ninety years old or more.

We will look at some examples from Jesus and His friends, but for the sake of a starting point, we will talk more about discovering the top five people I am already connected to. We will call these people your 2 a.m. people. The kind of people that you can rely on at inconvenient times.

Finally, and again, you will discover that clarity on any of these areas can happen in any order on your way to discovering your purpose. You may already know what you are passionate about, but a disconnect in the other three areas might have you in a space of feeling lost or unsure how to pursue your passions. On the road to discovering my purpose in Creation, I will need to define my passion; what really excites or motivates me? What are some things I enjoy doing that if I could get paid to do them, I would do those things with a sense of fulfillment and joy? (Purpose)

Let's begin with: Personality.

Personality

Have you ever lost a wallet, purse, or your phone? Maybe you dropped your debit/credit card or your ID. Even worse, you had one of those things stolen from you?

In any sense of the above, it's not a fun feeling.

Ranging from a sense of being inconvenienced to a feeling of dread or despair, the misplacing of valuable and invaluable things so closely associated to us as a person takes its toll.

One time, a friend of mine lost his wallet. Unable to find it, he gave up on its return. Until one day, it showed up in the mail! All of his cards, cash, ID card, and even his library card were there. The person who found it did not personally know my friend, so he sent it via the Post Office. My friend was so relieved!

I experienced a similar situation with a credit card. I used it at a gas station and forgot to stick it back in my wallet. Instead, I put it in my jacket pocket. When I was about to leave, it fell out! I did not notice its absence until the evening when I was at home. Retracing my steps, I called the gas station. Someone picked it up and handed it to the staff. They secured it in their safe for me to retrieve the next day!

The sense of relief we discover in times when something lost has been found hits everyone in a different way. Based on how valuable the lost thing is, the greater the joy when it is found.

This is what I think about whenever we begin to discover more awareness about our self or our "personhood."

When you think about YOU, what are some of the thoughts you have?

One of the early Christian church missionaries wrote about some of the distress he experienced when thinking about himself. He identified predominate urgencies at work within him. The things he longed to do, he often neglected, and the things he did not want to do were the things he kept on doing!

I believe the moment we begin to observe ourselves—our thoughts/feelings, our words, and our actions—is when we begin our journey toward a more flourishing and fulfilling life.

There's a reason why the self-help industry is one of the most lucrative. We are probably the only living species aware of our own faults and missteps. We pine over our insecurities or we ignore our negative feelings altogether.

When we look inward to better understand ourselves, based on how emotionally wounded we are, the harder it becomes to face those memories.

What we don't consciously realize is that the moments of our past and our conscious/subconscious responses to those moments are what form us as a person.

Just within the past twenty-five years, researchers have discovered that our bodies keep track of every emotionally-charged moment we experience. We may not be able to remember what we had for breakfast last week, but if you experienced a heightened emotional moment—a moment of emotional/physical trauma, a season of depression, a fight with a friend or partner, a sense of nirvana or bliss, whatever it was—our body keeps track of it.

Good, bad, or ugly, these moments cause massive chemical chain reactions in our brain. How we make sense of those moments will determine what those chemicals do to our body. Furthermore, what we do with the memories that get lodged in our brain will inform future responses to similar experiences.

All of these things we inherit from our parents (nature) and what we experience in our day to day living (nurture) add up to form our person (*ality*).

How our brains organize these events become the person we *are*.

Personality psychology theory has been around for a long time and has been called a number of different things. Trying to figure out why we do what we do is an ongoing conversation. This is largely due to the nuanced nature of human beings.

Ten people can witness and/or experience the same event while conveying ten different perspectives of what happened. Determining a consensus among the ten is easier than among a hundred or a thousand people.

We all respond differently to similar circumstances based on who we have become up until that point in time. How we respond to an experience as a teenager will probably differ from how we would respond to a similar experience as a parent of a teenager.

Life is crazy in that way.

Considering all of the different psychological, physiological, neurological, and biological influences of a person, people are similar in a lot of ways, but overall, we are all very different. We are each a unique person.

Our creative origin is similar. We are all of the same species, but unlike other animal species that are largely consistent in their behavior from group to group, our species can look and act juxtaposed to another group, even within the same city, club, or home!

We cannot better understand others until we have done the due diligence of looking at ourselves.

A wise teacher once explained that when looking or calling out something small in someone else's life, we must make sure we have dealt with the blatantly obvious thing we have neglected to address in ourselves.

Or as a number of different artists have claimed along the way, "Only God can judge me!"

It is easy to look at someone and think, "I know what's wrong with that person…" because it is difficult to look inward and face our own issues.

When it comes to our personality, a sign of maturity is a desire of looking inward to know ourselves, our tendencies, or our motivations. In discovering more about "why do I want to curse out the driver in front of me for only driving five mph over the speed limit in the passing lane on a highway?" and other motivating factors, we can grow as a person and see what the real issue is.

The same wise teacher even warned against assuming that while we think we have mastered some vice or negative action, the smallest form of it is just as egregious as its greatest version.

You may not have actually taken a life by murdering someone, but if you have thought negatively about a person, it's the same as murder.

According to this teacher, the thought of doing something is just as bad the action.

The teacher was not splitting hairs or debating the semantics of something, and the point of linking extremes was not for self-condemnation. The wise teacher spoke in this way to prevent our self-justification.

When we look inward at the motivations of our heart and mind, we grow to understand that other people are just like us, often doing the things they don't want to do. The wise teacher encouraged our inward considerations as a means to help us see each other as one humanity, a body of people, connected and moving toward a similar purpose.

This teacher lived during a time when war and violence was a cultural norm. The people group he was born into regularly held secret meetings to plot revenge against the governing body of the time. This group of subjugated people felt powerless and relied on dated prophecies promising a savior, a messiah, someone to deliver them from the throws of injustice they suffered on a daily basis.

This people group slowly grew impatient and bitter toward their rulers and each other. Within this people group, faction after faction formed to make a change. With every chance, they would cancel each other. Regularly, they would cut each other off from relationship and unity toward a common goal. Almost content on comparing themselves to others in hopes to not be as worse as their fellow countrymen, this people group became vindictive and judgmental.

In their innermost being, they were wounded people.

The same teacher born to this people group gave them hyperbolic examples, but never to make a point for the sake of making a point.

When it came to judging and condemning each other, the teacher asked why we look at the speck, the small thing in someone else's eye when we neglect to address the log in our own.

Whether it was the uncommon nature of the father with the wayward son to run after his returning son, a thought of murder, or failing to look at our log, the teacher didn't try to prove something. Instead he spoke to show a new way of being human. Perhaps, the only way of being truly human.

In these situations, they show us not only what needs to be done, but the way it is supposed to be done.

When tightening a lug nut or a screw (lefty loosey, righty-tighty), going too fast or using the wrong tool can strip the screw or nut. Going too far can get it lost or stuck.

When giving a compliment to someone, would you say it with a positive inflection or a disgruntled agitation?

Meditate and rid yourself of negative thoughts and emotions, but fail to refill yourself with positive truth statements, and you'll be left worse off than before.

"Pain that's not transformed is transmitted." - Richard Rohr

Wounded people, wound other people.

Healed people, help heal other people.

* * *

There's a way about all of us.

The way we dress.

The way we talk.

Eat.

Work.

Play.

Pray.

You could probably add more to this list.

There's "who you are…" [insert your name here].

Then there's "the way you are." It is hard to separate the "who" from the "way." Because in some form, the *way* you are makes up *who* people know you to be.

Way is different than "how." Unless it is 100 years from now and you were synthesized and grown in a lab or something, we all are aware of the "how humans are made."

The way you are is unique to you, which is influenced by countless inward and outward factors. Discovering the way you are *right now* matters. I cannot go back in time to change the way I did or said things in the past, probably things I wish I could redo, but I can become better so as to avoid doing those things in the future.

How do you discover why you are the way you are?

The long answer is 'counseling.'

What we cannot cover here, but would recommend everyone to do, is take stock of things you do, thoughts you think, the relationships you have had come and go, your day-to-day levels of motivation and/or hopeful outlook, and anything you wish you could change about yourself and write them down.

Seeing a counselor for an extended period of time will help you get to the core factors of those things. Furthermore, a counselor may also take this list and accompany with it a family genogram. A family genogram is a tool to help you identify familial impact on you as a person.

But none of that would help you right now. So, what is something you could do in the meantime while you work on the long term stuff?

Try a personality test.

And I am not talking about an internet-based "Which Harry Potter/Star Wars/Atlanta Real Housewives/etc. character am I?"

There are both printed and digital versions of researched based personality assessments. Some of the better ones are based on psychological principles from the likes of Freud, Jung, Piaget, Erikson, and Maslow. There are other notable psychologists too.

Different than neuroscience or biology, the science of psychology has a conflicted past.

We all do, don't we?

Psychology studies thoughts and their patterns, the conscious (things we are aware of), the subconscious (things we do without thinking about it), and the unconscious (dreams, sleeping, or invisible forces influencing us).

The mind is a tricky thing.

People have the capacity to lie, which makes the study of psychology even tougher. Research results can easily be skewed because of our propensity to alter the truth.

Self-deception is a real thing.

The ancient philosopher, Plato, considers it the worst kind of deception. Author Stephen King said we are the best at lying not to others, but to ourselves.

If I am not consciously aware of my tendencies, whether innocent in nature or atrocious, I leave myself open to all sorts of emotional and relational calamity.

My wife and I have a word for whenever we sense the other person or ourselves are not acting the way we should normally. We ask ourselves or the other person, "Am I hangry, right now?"

Or "Are you alright? Want to get something to eat?"

Have you ever been hangry? It's a fun way to describe the combination of being simultaneously "hungry" and "angry."

You know the feeling. Or you have experienced the wrath of someone who is hangry; they haven't eaten in a while or could use a pick-me-up and seem irritable. That's how our kids get. Whenever they're tired or hungry, they become different humans.

Pregnant women?

Never mind, I won't go there.

This similar sense of being *different than usual* stretches to stress, anxiety, depression, happiness, and euphoria. These moods or frames of mind seem like valley or mountain top moments.

What we tell ourselves about these moments form us as a person.

A personality exam is an entry level way for us to be honest about the way we respond to certain things. In the results, based on the driving factors behind the exam, we will be shown certain things about ourselves, thus allowing for more honesty within us.

Here are some of the better exams to take:

Myers-Briggs

Enneagram

DISC Assessment

CliftonStrengths

Big 5 Personality Traits

Taking multiple exams helps find consistencies among your responses to give you a more detailed picture of your tendencies.

All of these things, your life experiences, family history, genetics, worldview, and personality tendencies makeup the way you are as a person.

I recommend starting with your personality tendencies, instead of how you best relate with a higher-calling/being, your people/tribe, or your purpose, because the underlying common denominator in those areas is YOU.

I want to offer up a short explanation of how I visualize the sense of the question "where are you" with current GPS technology.

In GPS technology, three satellites send out spherical signals, while the device on our person has its own signal. The point where all the four signals intersect is where we are!

The three satellites are important, but if our signal isn't transmitting, we cannot rely on the other three signals to help us out. In effect, without our own signal, we are lost.

I say this not in an egocentric, all about ME kind of way, but in a

YOU are really important kind of way.

The Hebrew word for YOU is three letters.

The first letter of the Hebrew alphabet, which to them meant "beginning." The second letter is signifies the "end of all things." And the third is the letter for "breath."

The beginning and end of all things are in us.

YOU are important.

Finding *you* is probably the most important thing. In order to find YOU, there are three other signals we need to discover.

In Western thought, it's easier to think in a line. By beginning with YOU (yourself), it frees us up to move onto your pathway to God/the transcendent, then move to your people/tribe, and culminate with your passion/purpose what you have to give the world. In a way, these areas are spheres of influence in your life. They all impact the other. When all four intersect without disruption, that is where YOU are.

That is how this book is designed, but it doesn't necessarily happen in that order in real life.

There's a solid chance you have discovered breakthrough or clarity in one or more of these areas. The goal of this book is to help you have a better understanding of yourself in light of your origin story (where we come from), who are your people, and what brings you a sense of fulfillment.

If you are not content or expectant where you are in this season of life or in general, there's a solid chance these spheres of influence aren't intersecting in the way best meant for you. Or the way you're operating in one or more of these spheres lacks something significant.

Discovering and gaining a greater awareness of these four spheres and how they intersect has the potential to change everything about you and the places where you live, work, and play.

In the next chapter, we will continue with your pathway to God, higher-power, the transcendent thing you understand to be the backbone of our existence, etc.

Pathway

I have heard that you don't have to ask a person to declare what they believe, instead you should just *watch the way they live*. Look at their bank account and you'll see what they value. Listen to the way the talk and interact with others, and that will tell you a lot about a person.

I grew up in a Christian household. Within the Christian religion, there are a lot of different ways of expressing what one believes. There are a lot of differing beliefs and—an unnerving word—doctrines. When interacting with different people claiming to be following after this Christian religion, it has been common practice for people to ask other people, "What do you believe about …"

Salvation

Abortion

Sex

Gender

Violence

Politics

Money

Baptism

What I have found interesting about those interactions as I used to often participate in them—and much to my chagrin sometimes still do—is the people often talking are some of the least participatory people when it comes to living like a Christian-religion believer. I found it difficult to reconcile how this person was treating me with the love of Jesus they claimed to possess.

In a way, I don't say it as an inadvertent indictment of their actions, but as a confession, because I used to be that way. Once upon a time, I cared very much about being able to say what I believed and back it up with source material that the average person wouldn't care about.

What I remember about myself in those moments was my internal dialogue and the way I probably came across to the person directly involved in the conversation, and those indirectly involved that listened.

In those moments, I neglected relational thinking for right spoken doctrine. I was unkind. Unloving. Unlike Jesus.

Have you heard of the phrase, *people may not always remember what you said, but they will always remember how they felt when listening to you?*

I have had more than my fair share of feeling belittled by others and also my regretful belittling of others. What I discovered in some of these dehumanizing interactions was a gut-check. How I was interacting with God wasn't always translating to the way I was interacting with people.

Or, I was interacting with others based on my perceived interactions with God.

Here's the thing: what I believe about God will directly influence the way I interact with His creation.

If I believe God can be both good and (at least to my understanding) act in a way that doesn't seem "good," so too can I justify my actions in the name of others not rightly understanding my intentions.

If I believe God can murder humans, so too can I mistreat people and be at peace with it.

Naturally, there is a common pushback to this premise by well-read people. The pushback is "Well, we are all sinners, so we will usually fail and in no way does our failure represent God who is all truth and knowledge."

This is a true statement, but I do not believe this to be the "TRUTH." I get my basis for interpreting the nature of God by what I understand from the life of Jesus. In looking at what Jesus taught, did, and accomplished through His life, we get a clearer lens through which we can look at and connect with God's nature.

I don't know where you are in your faith journey, but I am convinced everyone believes in something. Whether it is one God (monotheism), many gods (polytheism), no gods (atheism), or a mixture of these three. In all three arenas arises a commonality: *faith in the sense of believing in something that provides meaning just because I believe in that thing.*

That was mouthful. Track with me here. If you made it this far in this book, then chances are, you are my mother (thanks for all of your support, Ma!) or you are intrigued by something in these pages. In either case, my submission to you is a question.

Whatever it is you believe in for a sense of meaning, how connected do you feel to it?

I (and billions of other people) believe in some form of a higher power. What that power is and one's experience of it varies from person to person. If you don't believe in some form of a higher power, you probably still believe in a way humans beings ought to interact with each other.

What if I told you that the goodness you believe in for another person is a law of nature programmed into us by a Creator God?

I believe it's only possible to feel connected with others or some form of duty toward another because of what lies within our genetic coding. For some reason, in spite of our brain's tendency to respond to many situations of fight, flight, or freeze, we find meaning and purpose in risking ourselves and our well-being for the sake of another.

Why is that?

Whatever the reason, it requires belief or faith for it to resonate within ourselves.

This leads me to another question: what are some activities or experiences you engage in that really make you feel "alive?"

What stirs your heart to hope or purpose for tomorrow?

Maybe in this season, you've lost sight of it. Hopefully the pathways we discuss here might rekindle some things for you.

Maybe you have discovered it, but feel disconnected. Maybe the things you used to enjoy don't cause the same enrichment of your soul.

Maybe you know the things that make you come alive or cause your heart to sing, or you walk in these pathways on a daily basis. Great! This is the goal.

Wherever you are in life as you read this chapter, I hope you discover, rediscover, or confirm the activities or experiences that help you feel connected to God.

Here's the thing,

God is real or He isn't.

If He isn't real to you and He's not real, then you're right. If He is real and isn't real to you, but you sense a connection to things beyond yourself, please accept my invitation to challenge yourself in asking this Creator God to reveal Himself in the things you enjoy and experience to enrich your life. If you are familiar with the life and way of Jesus, then there are some activities or experiences you may not find in those writings surrounding Jesus. If you have difficulty feeling connected to a

God-figure and those activities or experiences do not jive with the way of Jesus, then there's a chance you are working against the code of the universe.

A molecular metaphor for this would be the correct recipe of Hydrogen and Oxygen to make water. When you have the correct collision of molecules, two parts hydrogen and one part oxygen, you get water. Add another part oxygen and it becomes poisonous.

Sometimes, the things we think we enjoy—just because they're possible to experience—may be one or two molecular collisions off from being something healthy and/or life-giving. When we regularly interact with activities or experiences that are a degree or more off from an original intended experience, it can become dis-forming to our life, instead of transforming.

It's one thing to inhale dissipated vapors from certain incense, and another thing entirely to inhale vapors from tobacco.

That's just one example.

Some things are gonna help us feel more connected to God than other things. Based on my individual wiring, my biology, neurology, diet, cultural nurturing, etc., my personality and pathways to a "higher power" may differ in their expressions when compared to others.

Dominican Priest Herbert McCabe said it this way,

"The Jewish discovery that God is not a god but Creator is the discovery of absolute Mystery behind and underpinning reality. Those who share it (either in its Judaic or its Christian form) are not monotheists who have reduced the number of gods to one. They, we, have abolished the gods; there is only the Mystery sustaining all that is. The Mystery is unfathomable, but it is not remote as the gods are remote. The gods live somewhere else, on Olympus or above the starry sky. The Mystery is everywhere and always, in every grain of sand and every flash of color, every hint of flavor in a wine, keeping all these things in existence every microsecond. We could not literally approach God or get nearer to God for God is already nearer to us than we are to ourselves. God is at the ultimate depth of our beings making us to be ourselves."

Based on your background, there may be some triggering lines in there. For clarity, Herbert isn't advocating for Animism or a sense of Deism. If anything, he brings into focus an invitation to shift our awareness of God's closeness. It is natural for us as humans to want to understand God in knowable terms. God is both knowable by experience and mysterious in His vastness. The tension is to recognize both are true. In this opening ourselves to a renewed sense of awe and wonder toward God, we free ourselves to be free with Him in walking out the intention for humankind: faith, hope, love, honor, and service.

Let's outline the common pathways discussed and adopted by other researchers, teachers, etc. There are multiple ways to discuss these different themes for connection, both in the activities themselves or activities more associated with someone's predominant personality.

The following was put together by professor, Keas Keasler[2]. It is a mixture of activities and how they relate to common predominant personality traits. Take a look:

A Naturalist *feels closest to God in the out-of-doors, in the midst of creation. Whether it's the mountains, forest, or ocean, being in nature awakens this person to God's presence and beauty. Examples are Saint Francis and the poet Elizabeth Barrett Browning who wrote, "Earth's crammed with heaven, and every common bush afire with God; but only he who sees, takes off his shoes – the rest sit around and pluck blackberries."*

A Traditionalist *loves God through the historic dimensions of the faith like rituals, symbols, and liturgy. This person would probably enjoy praying the Psalms, following fixed-hour prayer, and celebrating all the seasons of the Christian calendar. One contemporary example is the Episcopalian writer Phyllis Tickle, who compiled the Divine Hours prayer books.*

A Contemplative *seeks God through quieter disciplines such as solitude, meditation, and journaling. A biblical example of this is Mary of Bethany, who sat in adoration at Jesus' feet and was commended by Jesus for doing so. This person can relate to the 16th century monk, Saint John of the Cross, who said, "Silence is God's first language."*

A Visionary *loves God by dreaming a great dream and setting out to accomplish it. This person feels God's presence and delight as he uses his gifts for the kingdom. John Wesley, the founder of the Methodist church, is an example, as is William Carey, the mission-*

ary pioneer to India. He once said, "*Expect great things from God. Attempt great things for God.*"

A Socialite *connects with God best around other people, journeying with and confiding in them. For this person, community plays a vital role in experiencing God's presence, and she is inspired by the example of the early church in Acts 2 sharing life with one another. Those with this personality type often gravitate toward more intimate settings for living out the faith such as small groups, close-knit friendships, and mentoring relationships.*

An Intellectual *loves God through using his mind to think deeply about God and matters of theology. For this person, "faith" is something to be understood as much as experienced. One example is C. S. Lewis, who said his heart came alive whenever he was working through a tough bit of theology with a pipe in his teeth and a pencil in his hand.*

A Caregiver *loves God by being compassionate and loving others even if it means significant sacrifice. This person believes she is serving Christ when she serves those who are in need, and she finds the act to be energizing rather than draining. Perhaps the supreme example of this is Mother Teresa who founded the Missionaries of Charity.*

A Worshiper *experiences God through joyful celebration and music. This person wants to linger in the awe, beauty, and splendor of God, and loves to express adoration for him through songs or art. The hymn writer, Charles Wesley, is an example, as are the modern song writer Rich Mullins and visual artist, Makoto Fujimura.*

An Activist *is at war with injustice and loves God by fighting it. This person is compelled by a vision of the world where God's Kingdom is fully present, and feels he must stand up for the marginalized and confront those who oppress others. A few examples are William Wilberforce, Martin Luther King Jr., and Shane Claiborne.*

After reading the list, there ought to be a one or two that resonate with your inner being. By resonate, I mean you read something and it peaked a sense of interest or self-identification such as "This sounds like me."

There's a line in the Old Testament of the Bible with songs, poems, and ascents; and the writer said, "Deep calls to deep in the roar of your waterfalls; all your waves and breakers have swept over me."

That line is thought to be written by someone who had been driven out of their homeland, cut off from their people, and are calling out to who they know to be their Higher Power; the same God we have previously mentioned in this book.

Sometimes in these ancient writings, what wasn't intended explicitly for us in the text may be able to be interpreted implicitly by readers thousands of years later. There may have been a specific reason and truth for the writer of that line. For us, we can read something like that, couple it with information gathered with modern technology, and then draw out an unintended nugget of truth.

This is important because there is something we have learned about the spectrum of sound involving waterfalls. Simply, our human senses have their limitations. There are way more colors than what our eyes can see and brain interpret. There are also sounds our ears are not capable of hearing.

When it comes to the analyzed sound of waterfalls, the noise hits on each end of the human's ability to hear. Meaning, from the highs to the lows of what we are capable of hearing, and everything in between, that is the sound of a waterfall. The same goes for the sound of rain and the crashing of breaking waves.

The writer, who calls out to God for His waves to sweep over him, recognized a deep pain requiring a deep healing. For the writer, the depth of the need is met by the fullness of his God. No matter where we are on the "spectrum" of hearing, this God's voice hits on all the levels.

An implicit and unintended message from the writer to us is one of the "call." There are a number of places in the ancient writings about the need for reminders. Several stories have the people setting up a system of reminders in order to reconsider their Creator and His intention for His people.

What if, in the coding of what we know to be reality there are fixed points of reference or constants to consider. When we hear the sound of a waterfall, the rain, or waves crashing against the shore, we can leverage those as reminders there might actually be a Creator wanting to connect with His creation.

The positive effects of these noise phenomenon on us as humans is almost universal. Barring deafness or chemical imbalance, many of us are sensitive to certain sounds. The sounds of waterfalls, rain, and crashing waves causes an increase in a certain brainwave that promotes a sense of peace or calmness in us. It settles the brain to a state of *rest*.

This is why it is important to discover our primary pathway in which we best connect with the Divine. If God is there, then He is calling to you in a way that most resonates within your being.

Another ancient writer whose words were collected in the same Old Testament book as the one writing about waterfalls said, "He leads me beside the waters of rest. He restores my soul; He leads me in the paths of righteousness for His name's sake."

In this ascent, the writer said "paths of righteousness." Without over-simplifying, the word righteous means "right standing;" to be in a right relationship with something or someone.

If you have ever been wronged in a relationship or have wronged someone, then you know the different steps they or you had to take in order to make things right again. With the writers in the Old Testament, they and their ancestors, time and again, acted in selfish ambition and ignorance, breaking down their relationship with the Creator.

For God, He wants us to feel at rest, to know by experience where we stand with Him. For the sake of humanity, this God took it upon Himself to make the relationship right, to stop at nothing to convince humanity of His love. He is nothing like the ancient gods of legend and myth that required human sacrifice or to hate other people. He is nothing like the people who lord over and abuse people for their own gain.

This God wants His people to be at rest.

For the ancient people hearing news like this would have been scandalous—to some degree. They had it in their minds this God also had to be appeased by violence.

We aren't faced with this same urgency in our times. If anything, there is a growing resignation for believing in a form of God-being. Partly due to the story and accomplishments of Jesus Christ and partly due to the vast separation from that worldview system where people believed in all sorts of gods and feared wronging them. People are not less spiritual, they are just more open to the idea of a universal being of consciousness and goodwill toward others.

What if this universal being of consciousness and goodwill toward others actually originated with God and was lost in our interpretation of what has been said of God or done "in His Name?"

The God of this Creation is one of love, goodness, mercy, graciousness, "slow to anger," and faithfulness.

He wants that Truth to settle in our beings; to be established and built upon. Due to the infinite nature of His being, He chooses to find ways to express this truth in all sorts of experiences and utilizing all sorts of people too.

Sometimes when we feel stuck in our lives, it's good to double check how we have sought to connect with our Creator and rediscover those ways and experiences that bring our minds and beings to a state of rest, a sense of meaning, and a heart posture of purposeful living.

* * *

One of the ancient teachings still talked about today is our creative sensibilities, and how they are expressed uniquely in our being alive.

God created humankind in His image.

He is also recorded as saying it is not good for His image-bearing creation to be in isolation, separated physically, emotionally, and spiritually from other image-bearing creations.

Simply put, people need people.

Truth is, we need each other.

The definition of our being isn't in the illusion of our autonomy, nor is it solely in bearing the image of our Creator. The sum of what makes you, "YOU," is in the competing tensions of self, our eternal origin, other people, and what we have to give the world.

This too is the overarching mystery of what Christians try to explain regarding God, His Holy Spirit, and Jesus.

For thousands of years, people have studied the things of God—called Theology—to interpret and convey the reality of God, how He came to the earth in the flesh as a human named Jesus, and articulate this Holy Spirit that was promised to exist in and around humans and guide them into heaven-on-earth-things.

The phenomenon of one God in three "persons" is almost as distracting as it is important to making sense of the connectivity of all things in our reality. To try and explain how God, Jesus, and the Holy Spirit are one but not the same is quite impossible. However, it is something that underlies Christian teachings. We cannot explain it, but we can experience it.

To believe in one God expressed in three distinct persons is, in a way, to acknowledge and pursue an understanding of the interconnectedness of all things.

My thoughts, behavior, genetics, diet, relationships, farming practices, the economy, government, welfare, healthcare, cultural expressions, climate, geography, infrastructure, along with other' thoughts, behaviors, genetics, diet, etc. are all strung together somehow.

To connect with a higher being who is expressed and experienced in different ways provides a lens through which we can reorient our individualized selves within the collective makeup of the whole.

This leads me to our next sphere: people. The ones we know, the ones we interact with, the ones who left, the ones we haven't met yet, and the ones we'll never meet. Everything in our intuitive-survival instincts tell us to be cautious and self-protective around other people while research and wisdom tell us the counterintuitive posture toward others of generosity and service more often than not leads to a long, healthy, and fulfilling life.

See you on the next page.

People

―――・・●・・―――

Have you ever felt like you as a person were "spread too thin?"

Like there isn't enough time for you, let alone the other people in your life?

I have been there.

So has Michael Keaton, who once was described as "a man who never has enough time for the things he wants to do is offered the opportunity to have himself duplicated."

Hold on, that might have been a movie, not real life…but you and I live in real life.

And I bet we have shared the same thought:

"A couple more of me would be helpful."

As a husband and a father, I wish I had more time to do all the things I want to do *and* spend time with the people I love.

This is on top of the other things demanding my time; work, volunteering, church activities, kid's activities, and random things I want to experience.

What I have discovered was not that I needed more time, but the acceptance of my limitations. There is only one version of me. I am not meant to do this life alone.

Research has shown Americans are some of the loneliest people in the world. It further found that women are more likely to report this phenomenon while men are less likely to acknowledge their loneliness.

People reporting higher than average social media usage are twice as likely to report feeling lonely.

It's time we become honest with ourselves.

An eighty yearlong Harvard study found that "embracing community helps us live longer, and be happier."

In a significantly large test group, the number one commonality amongst people living past the age of 90 wasn't genetics or diet, but the presence of close friends.

In a separate study, researchers looked into the exceptional health of a towns' residents in Pennsylvania.

The town is called Roseto.

Even before the research study, folks in the area became aware of the peoples' exceptional good health and longer than average life spans in comparison to surrounding towns. Researchers looked into reasons why the people were significantly healthier than others. Naturally, they looked at the diet for the average citizen:

"The town of largely Italian immigrants smoked unfiltered stogies, drank copious amounts of wine, largely neglected the drink-

ing of milk and soft drinks while skipping out on the popularized Mediterranean diet in favor of meatballs and sausages fried in lard accented with hard and soft cheeses."

My aortic valve gurgled when I first read this.

They looked at their diet and then the peoples' employment. They couldn't find any correlation signifying their diet or line of work to their health. What they found was similar to the findings of the Harvard study, and it had little to do with their diet, employment, economic status, or demographic background.

What they found were shared generational connections and relationships. In this town, they all knew each other. They visited each other's places of business, regularly spent time with one another, and went to church with one another.

They did a lot of the same things with the same people.

We know diet matters. Your financial well-being matters. Your genetics matter. We know being alone or isolated is poor on your health.

But what if there is something worse than being alone or isolated?

It's feeling like you're alone in a crowded room.

In your life you are surrounded by people, but you're not surrounded by relationships.

What made the people of Roseto so unique?

Everybody looked out for everybody.

Where did this "everyone looking out for everyone" come from?

Is it possible to have this type of community mindset in the 21st century?

This book was published after the initial events of the COVID-19 pandemic, disheartening racial tensions, and political unrest. The rate of division seemed to be increasing at an insurmountable rate.

A similar thing happened within the community of Roseto. As the older generations eventually passed away, the sense of shared connection, their immigration journey from Italy to a foreign land and working together to make a living, died with them. With each passing generation, collectivism, unity, and intentional community dissolved.

Now, Roseto is much like many other rural communities in the United States. Overall health and life expectancy has dropped to national averages. Their sense of collectivism has turned to hyper-individualism.

What if we could shift our focus just a little bit and find that sense of community again?

I think it's possible to find your people and give yourself and ultimately "us," the opportunity to live a full and flourishing life.

I cannot be me,

without you.

What if there is a blueprint for our designated makeup? I mean something within God that explains why we benefit from authentic unified relationships with other people?

Let's go back to the ancient writings as recorded in the first book of the Bible.

"Then God said, "Let US make man in our image, after our likeness."

I want to focus on the last word, "likeness."

Likeness is the nature or personality of the inspiration for the creation.

Up until now, we have looked at the four disrupted spheres as described in the ancient account of Genesis.

We want to grow in self-awareness and we want to grow in our relationship with our Creator. What I am proposing in this chapter is the idea that other people are pertinent to us better knowing ourselves and encountering our Creator in a face to face kind of way.

Fundamentally, all people are created equal and express—in their own unique way—the image of the Creator.

Unfortunately, not all people have been given equal opportunity to be fully human.

What if I saw my individualism as a chance to bless the collective whole?

My experience in this life is intimately personal, but my overall growth is intrinsically communal.

Who are your people?

Who are the people you are connected with that bring the best of you out into the world?

There are a number of ways you can identify who are your people. Social media has muddied the waters a bit when it comes to connecting with others. We are able to collect a large amount of digital connections in a single location that supersedes the amount of in-person interactions we experience on a daily basis. When we look at the things people post online and then interact with those posts, it signals a similar—but less intense—feeling of connection. There's nothing inherently wrong with social media. Like many other technological advances, it's a tool for communication.

It becomes a problem when it entirely replaces our in-person interactions.

The key there is *entirely*.

Social media and the Internet are tools to be leveraged for bridging gaps or maintaining connections. It cannot be the *whole* connection. Eventually, it all needs to come together *in-person*.

The over-arching purpose of this book is to guide you in the right direction of becoming aware of your proximity with yourself, your Creator, your people, and your purpose. This book is very much a proposal for reorienting yourself to where you are, right now. There are other more in-depth tools to seek after this book, none of which I have personally developed.

However, for the sake of this chapter, I will do my best to help on how you self-identify your people.

I want to lean on something Jesus modeled perfectly with *His people*.

Who were His people?

For the sake of this instruction, we will say His people were the twelve disciples. They were the ones regularly mentioned and the ones allowed consistent and close proximity to Jesus.

He also had an even closer inner circle, they were people who got even more time with Him.

Jesus had a best friend. Scholars believe it was a guy named John, who wrote the Gospel of John and some other books in the New Testament.

Then there were James and Peter. These three had the most access to Jesus. From there, it's unknown how the other 4-12 guys connected with Jesus. Beyond the twelve, there were other disciples (including many women) who followed Jesus around but weren't considered a part of the inner twelve.

For us, these people may be co-workers, parents of our kids' friends, people we see at church or other community based gatherings, etc. You know a lot of their names, but the amount of personal information you've shared with those people is considerably less compared to those closer to you.

The average middle-aged man has only one close friend beyond their significant other. Women will cite three to seven close friends.

How many do you have?

Use this definition of a *best, inner circle, or close friend*: *they are someone you see on a consistent basis, you talk about things beyond surface level conversation, are able to share deeply personal things, and are willing to be there for each other at times when others might not be there.*

Outside of your significant other, do you have a best friend?

_____

How about 1-2 inner circle friends?

_____   _____

How about 1-2 other close friends?

_____   _____

What was the level of difficulty in filling those blanks? If it was easy, then there's a strong chance you have more. It is possible to have a plethora of relationships, but there really should only be a single digit amount of people who have special access to you. Anything beyond that becomes too difficult to sustain. Remember, we are limited.

The key starting point to being in right relationship with other people is to know the people you are already in relationship with. Once you've successfully identified those people, the work begins to be as intentional with those people as you possibly can.

Are the people on your list safe?

Do you trust them with your dreams?

Do they have the permission to ask you the hard questions about your life?

Do you have open spaces to add someone to your circle?

The key here is to still begin with those you are in relationship with and ensure you're making a consistent effort to nurture those relationships. While you do that, begin to think of people you wanted to put there but it didn't feel right to do so. I would start by asking them to be more intentional with you. That might sound weird, but sometimes we do so much assuming with others (and talking around things) that we disqualify people based on our own internal dialogue, indirectness, and self-doubt.

Seriously, if you have open spaces, then there's probably 1-2 peoples' names you wanted to write down. Go talk to them. Explain to them what you're doing and how you want to surround yourself with the right people. Put yourself out there. They might surprise you. Then when this new intentionality is forged, be there for them and allow them into your life to also be there for you.

You cannot be you without them and they cannot be them without you. Think healthy interdependence and not codependence.

This life we live is best done together.

Real relationships aren't a casual thing.

They're intentional. We ought to value this. If I am being intentional with my close people, then when they're around me, I can believe they are being intentional too! They think of me. They remember things. They ask questions. They not only want to be seen and heard, they want me to feel that way too.

There's life in it!

But Nolan, what if I have I tried and have been betrayed? I have put myself out there and only get hurt over and over again.

I would tell you that if the Creator put Himself out there to be received or rejected and that the bent of this creation is toward connection, then it's up to you to believe or not believe God will continue to bring opportunities your way.

The key is knowing what to look for.

A solid follow-up resource to consider is a book written by a Psychologist, Dr. Henry Cloud. The title of the book is "Boundaries: When to Say Yes, How to Say No to Take Control of Your Life"

Here's the thing, we often don't realize how important community is until it happens to us. Some of us haven't been in real community before, so we don't know what it looks like.

If God is real and He created you and me, then this life is not to be enjoyed by one's self, but to be lived out with each other.

Let's move on to the next chapter to discuss our gifting, as in, what you and I have to offer the world.

Purpose

Almost all stories follow a simple path from start to finish:

1) **Introduction.** This is where we learn who the main protagonist and/or antagonist are. We learn a bit about their world, what goes on around the characters, and the setup.

2) **Inciting Incident.** Also known as the conflict. We are presented with the problem. Maybe it is a tragic story with the main character's conflicting moral compass. It could be an evil enemy threatening to destroy everything the main character would die to defend. This is the part where the story really gets interesting. It is expected, but necessary. All the best stories have a great tension that must be waded in and prevailed against.

3) **Progressive Complication.** This is the point of the story where we hope the protagonists will succeed on their first try. If the hero or heroine won on their first time against the thing they are trying to defeat, it would make for short books and movies. The progressive complication of the story is where the main characters try and fail again and again. We notice the

flaws in their personalities and decision-making. The characters become "human" through their struggle. It is in their failing that they become relatable.

4) **Turning Point/Climax.** Finally, the protagonists are getting their stuff together. Often, a guide will come along during the progressive complication and the main characters won't listen. Finally, as our beloved characters learn and grow, often by obeying what the guide instructs, the story gets a fresh breath of hope.

5) **Resolution/Moral Of The Story.** Also known as the "most debated part of the story." Many of us form our opinions of how a story should end. The longer the story goes on and evolves from book to book, movie to movie, and season to season, the greater the anticipation to end it the way we want it to end. Resolution and moral of the story could easily be their own parts of a story. Depending on how the story is told, we get the moral of the story during the resolution. Sometimes, the moral of the story can stand on its own.

Have you ever thought about your life in the form of a story still being written?

If so, great! If not, track with me.

The story of the two sons is also known as a "parable." Like a wise saying or a problem, the point of the story is rarely about the things in the story so much as it is about the thing behind the story.

Oftentimes parabolic stories and narratives are not about the characters but about those listening to it. The ancient teacher (Jesus) would follow up these parables with "let those who have ears hear." Basically, either get the meaning or you don't. Parables humble the wise and edify the foolish.

Stories connect us.

They connect us to things beyond ourselves. Simultaneously, they reflect the state of our inner being. They incite us to reflect on our lives.

Who am I?

Why am I here?

Where am I going?

How will I get there?

A great story brings about questions for us to consider. The goal is to ask the right questions because not all questions are created equal.

Consider the following question:

Do you want to have a fulfilling and flourishing life?

I hope to live such a life.

My life hasn't always been as full or overflowing as I wanted it to be. Even still, as I type this, I am learning what a full life looks and feels like. Your answer to the question may be a simple "yes!" I want it, but don't think I have it. Where one thinks they have it, another is focused on how they don't have it. In those cases, they may never find it.

I started this chapter about 'purpose' this way for a reason;

The moment you discover what you purpose to be and do in life is when this whole living experiment becomes real.

Did you catch that?

When *you* discover what *you purpose to be and do*...

I recall one of my favorite authors—Donald Miller—talking about this same idea of writing a memoir of sorts in his book, *A Million Miles in a Thousand Years*—and I am paraphrasing from memory—"the life an author lives versus the life they write about often don't align." Based on inspiration from a friend and fellow author of Don's, he recalled meeting Bob Goff and learning how

Bob lives the type of life Don wished he was living.

Note the present tense, "lives."

It happens to me whenever I read an engaging story, memoir, or watch a movie. I get wrapped up in the narrative, I become complicit to the scenes, dialogue, and emotions of the characters. I involve my story in something or someone else's narrative.

Many of us do it.

Even in life, we subconsciously sort ourselves, others, and God into roles like hero, victim, guide, villain, or an extra.

For a long time, I wondered if my involvement in other peoples' stories was a way of avoiding the manifestation of my life's purposefulness.

Unfulfilled by a number of things in my life, I took interest in all sorts of other narratives. Instead of unpacking my backstory and purposefully developing or participating in my character arc, I often found ways to escape the responsibility of my present-future.

If you're like me and a fan of cinema, then you are familiar with the telling of a character's back story. It can be conveyed in all sorts of creative ways, but the purpose is the same; it portrays and explains why the character in the current events of the film's story do what they do, talk the way the talk, and think the way they think.

It's a way of explaining what really makes up a person and their experiences, their family, and their skills and talents. What's their core motivation?

This question—in all of its forms (interchanging the topics of purpose, meaning, destiny, etc.)—have been wrestled with by humans for thousands of years. Just within the past 100 years, we have seen many doctors of Psychiatry advocate for "the pursuit of meaning" being the actual motivation for everyone. *What is the point to all of this?*

What does it all mean?

Our search for *meaning*.

Earlier, I argued that a fulfilling life is finding our rhythm or being in right relationship with four key spheres; ourselves and our tendencies, higher power/Creator/God, who are the people in my corner, and lastly, my purpose or gifting.

The key Psychiatrist advocating for this emphasis on meaning is Viktor Frankl. He proposed the theory of meaning being our primary motivation. If his theory is true, then we can at least pursue the thought that this must come from somewhere. At least, in so many words, that is how I laid out the small case for having a source from which we were created.

If we were created, then a logical progression to pursue is the meaning to why the Creator put us here, in our reality, to exist and live.

There has to be meaning for all of the suffering.

There has to be a point!

Instead, what if the point is living our life in enjoyment of what the Creator put in us as a reflection of the Creator's being?

The Creator took from Himself and made Humankind.

What if that's the point?

What if the point is to take from ourselves and give it for the sake of others?

Everything else is just window dressing.

What is the thing we are supposed to give?

I believe each person has some expression within them that is meant to bless, serve, and love others.

I love watching the Olympic Games, both Summer and Winter games. I don't watch every sport, but whenever it's on, I am in awe of how effortless the contestants make the game appear. I have heard the jokingly submitted proposal of at least one average person needs to participate in each activity to further show how difficult are the skills on display by the elite athletes. It would make for some interesting television!

It has taken some time to see it, but I look for those moments whenever someone is really in their element. They are doing something they really enjoy. They don't have to be amazing at it, but you might know what I am talking about.

Back in college, I helped out with the Special Olympics of Illinois. The State competition was held at Illinois State University. During one of the basketball games, a team needed to pass the ball from out of bounds in bounds and go on offense. Well, all of the players took off down the court, leaving the ref and the player out of bounds all alone. They called to the closest player and told them to go back and receive the inbounds pass.

The player turned around, and upon comprehending what was being asked, the smile on their face doubled in size. Pointing to themselves, they exclaimed, "ME?!" They came alive with a sense of belonging and purpose. They could not fathom the invitation to do something that to you and me might seem like a small deal, receive the inbounds pass, and dribble the ball on the court, but to them, we may have just asked them to carry the Olympic Torch to the tippy top to light the flame.

I have seen this time and again in all sorts of people doing all sorts of disciplines. It's like they are there in front of you, doing their thing, but you notice their mind is really far away from them. Physically they're still there, but their soul is becoming one with something; it went somewhere as they got lost in doing the thing they love doing.

Some even call this kind of harmonizing with their craft *the flow state*.

I want to draw our attention back to the ancient writings of Genesis.

"God created man in His own image; He created him in the image of God; He created them male and female God blessed them, and said to them, "Be fruitful, multiply, fill the earth, and subdue it. Rule the fish of the sea, the birds of the sky, and every creature that crawls on the earth." Genesis 1:27-28

Here, we see the Creator-God give man a list of five things to do. It begins with the phrase, "Be fruitful…"

Personally, I like this mandate because I enjoy eating fruit more than I enjoy eating vegetables.

Who's with me?

If you are child still living at home and reading this, next time your parents ask you to eat all of your vegetables, quote Genesis 1:28. "Be fruitful!" Why are all these brussel sprouts on my plate? God didn't tell us be brussel sprouts!

I get it, I don't care for brussel sprouts, but I digress.

What we see here in Genesis is *action and duty*. It is tempting to look at this list of five things and think to do them in order as they're listed. In a way, it kind of makes sense to consider it in that way.

It's hard to rule something before you subdue it. It's hard to fill if we haven't multiplied.

I don't want to get bogged down in the philosophical or logistical components of this five-fold mandate. For the sake of this chapter, I will focus on the phrase, "be fruitful."

What does it mean to be fruitful?

The Hebrew word here means "to blossom, bear fruit, posterity, fruitful vine."

I joked a moment ago about preferring fruit to vegetables. Other than taste, I never really paid attention to the differences in fruits and veggies.

What sets them apart is that one produces seeds and the other is more associated with being roots.

To be fruitful means to produce something that produces something. However, a fruit cannot grow and produce the seed without being established by a root.

It's possible to get these things out of order. There is something here, though; in what God put us on this earth to BE and DO.

Based on your generational influences, each of us may have a different definition on what it means to work and be a positive contributor to society. Somewhere along the way, between the mandate in Genesis and our contemporary cultural context, emerged this idea:

We work to live.

This reminds me of the song Working For the Weekend. For many of us, we have worked jobs we don't like because it pays the bills and puts food on the table. Based on your upbringing, getting to enjoy your work was something reserved for the lucky few. The rest of us have to work and do whatever it takes so we can make ends meet.

I want to submit for your consideration that the God in Genesis created us for work.

We live to work.

This is our purpose. Don't groan too much or drop this book off at your nearest Goodwill Donation Center. Unfortunately, the intention for work got messed up as described in the third chapter of Genesis. Furthermore, cultural, governmental, and economical influences have constructed a worldview for us that work is something we "have to do," but enjoying it is left to the lucky few.

Ultimately, to live with our purposefulness in mind, is to ask yourself, "Am I doing something I am passionate about that blesses someone else, and if so, is it producing the fruit I want to see?"

In other words, am I doing things that really matters for myself or others?

What are somethings that when you do them, even if you're physically and emotionally tired at the end of the day, was worth doing anyways?

Let me put it this way; there are days I am tired, but when I look back at my day, I become excited by everything I accomplished. There are other days I am exhausted and after reflecting on it, I noticed I accomplished little. I did a bunch of things I really don't care to do on a regular basis.

I would guess most of us feel exhausted a lot of the time because we are doing things we really would prefer to not do. Many of us are working for the weekend. Working so we don't have to.

What if you could work in such a way that you looked forward to it?

What a dream right?

Plenty of self-help gurus out there promises that it's possible.

Sure, in a way it is. However, it's unlikely. Unless you are willing to do whatever it takes to create such a purpose filled life for yourself. My apologies, but that's not what this book is all about. There are other ones out there helping in this particular area.

What I am trying to unpack here is the necessity to assess what are the things I am passionate about?

Are there ways that my passions can positively impact others?

If I am regularly frustrated, discontent, or feel like something is missing, then maybe it's time to reassess the things I do on a regular basis. Sometimes, we can get so self-involved or so "family-focused" that we neglect to really identify what "makes me come alive?"

What if billions of people lived out their passions in a way that positively benefited other people? What would become of the world and culture?

Recently, I heard a story about a retired couple with solid pensions whom answered what they sensed to be a call from God to move back to their home town. The town is economically shattered and the crime rate there is quite high. Many high school students would get moved from grade level to grade level without ever scoring close to their peers. This was something unique to this school district—many Juniors and Seniors in High School with grade school level reading skills. It was truly a rough situation.

This couple felt a sense from God to move home and serve their community. And that's what they did. Despite the odds and lack of optimism from school officials, this couple—in just a sixty-day period—worked with students (without any financial assistance besides their retirement fund) to raise many of their reading levels to that of a Freshman or Sophomore. Each day, the couple is exhausted by the amount of initiatives they've added since their initial success. But they're not tired. Whatever they touch has been turning to gold for these students. This couple wakes up energized to go and do it again.

There have been set backs. It's not all green lights. There have been failures, but they discovered something that even in "retirement," helps move others forward to a better tomorrow.

When was the last time you seriously assessed your passions, your gifting, in order to be more purposeful with your time and resources?

Where are you in the formation of your story? What are the stories people will tell about you after you're gone? Not everyone who pursues their passion or gifting will become nationally famous, but that's not why we do it.

We need more of us discovering our purpose and our gifting. As each person discovers this and seeks ways to leverage it for the positive impact of others, the better off we will be as a humanity.

A couple solid assessments/resources to use in this pursuit are:

freeshapetest.com - trumotivate.com - careertest.com

Another way of looking at your purpose is through the lens of stewardship. The five things directed by the Creator is a broad stroke of stewardship. Since we don't have a choice in being brought into this world, it is up to us on how we choose to respond to this opportunity of being alive. Hence, the pursuit of purpose and meaning.

Through the worldview lens of stewardship, it differs slightly in the binary approach of ownership and renting.

In our Western Culture, we put a large emphasis on ownership. Conversely, I have read a number of articles published in 2020 & 2021 about a case for owning as little as possible and only borrowing or renting when you need things.

These are solid cases for both sides.

Stewardship is unique because in it, you treat everything like you own it, but with the humility of the fact it was given to you by somewhere else. I think of a "self-made" person as a myth. Even in the spirit of the title of: working hard, determination, and grit; the whole idea is illogical. Especially as we have laid it out here over the course of the book. It's more like "we-made" people.

To walk in one's gifting or purpose is to walk in such a way their interactions with everything ought to be that of stewardship.

Your family.

Friends.

Co-workers.

Job.

House.

Hobbies.

Conversations.

Mental health.

Finances.

We are owners of nothing, but stewards of everything.

The better we steward these things, the more akin we are to fulfilling the five-fold directive given by the Creator. The better stewards we become, the more our lives will flourish.

Just a few chapters left, and I am going to lean more heavily into the worldview of God, Jesus, and the Holy Spirit. If that's of interest to you to see how these things connect, then stay tuned! If not, you caught the gist of this book in the first eight chapters. There's more to this, but I cannot go much further without a deep connection to this particular worldview.

From here, I will speak to the idea of "process." The goal is a harmonization of these four spheres: Pathway, Personality, People, and Passion. Discovery, planting, growth, maturity, and bearing fruit requires time and effort.

It's all process.

However, in our rapid culture, it is easy to become disillusioned with the process and patience therein.

I will touch on the importance of setting up healthy rhythms as you begin to assess those spheres and self-determine what your next steps might be. In that chapter, we will put emphasis on prioritizing intentional times of rest and respite.

Simplifying our lives allows us to do less, but do those things with more excellence. Instead of finding time to do more things, what would it look like to simplify and become hyper-focused with our time? Then, we can give more of ourselves to those times of work because we know we are setting aside time each week to disconnect and rest.

We'll close the book with some parting thoughts and an invitation.

(W)Here You Are & How To Get (T)Here

Okay, let's assume you have read this far and are not totally tuned out to the idea that "Hey, maybe there's something here. I am going to determine how I best connect with my Creator, myself, others, and my gifting."

Once you have identified those things, then what?

Now it's time to do something about it. However, this book will not possess those particular answers pertaining to your specific position as they relate to those four things. However, what I can give you are some guiding principles and reminders to reference as you continue on your journey.

The purpose of the question "Where are you?" is to ask yourself, where am I in relation to God, myself, others, and my gifting…

In this season of your life.

Where is "here?"

This is important because there are so many things vying for our attention on a daily basis. Research in the 1970's determined the average person received 500 or so different marketing messages per day.

In 2022? That number is closer to 5,000-10,000 messages per day. If you have ever felt like it's impossible to get ahead, that you're constantly trying to catch up to some elusive sense of peace, then there's a chance you too have fallen victim to this sense of plurality.

Too many things, too little time.

Even some of the most organized people I personally know have self-identified with too much on their plate. They have fully leveraged time-saving and organizational help tools to add more to their lives, instead of less. It's crazy!

There's a healthy tension to walk with the way we live our lives.

Naturally, for the sake of expelled energy and whenever it is possible to conserve said energy, our brains will simplify things into as few choices as possible. Things take on an either/or basis for decision-making. It's the disillusioned lens of two choices; good or bad, hot or cold, day or night, right or wrong, life or death, etc.

There's more, but you get the idea, there's a lot of things we engage with on a daily basis, which involves a sense of obvious division of choices. I get it. If you think about it, when we boil most of our decisions down, we are usually left with two things to choose from. And that's OK!

However, as you and I both know, there's a lot of gray area. Thinking in black and white seems easy at first, but time and again, we are faced with dilemmas of choice. The more we acknowledge the nuance of this life, the way everything seems to be connected to everything else, and the sooner we can give up a sense of trying to control things outside of our control, the more free we become.

What is within our control, is how we choose to respond in relation to the four main spheres laid out in this book. The trick is to not get caught up on whatever it is you decide to do next, whether it is the right or wrong decision.

Oftentimes, we will wrestle with choices through a primary lens of:

What is the *right* choice, here?

I think it would distract from the point to succinctly lay out my case for the following question, but I will ask it anywyay. Here is the question for you to engage with:

What if we thought less about whether something is right or wrong?

Instead, what would it look like to shift our self-assessment to something like;

will this decision or choice impact my life for the better?

What if I chose to see every life step I take as another opportunity for growth, regardless of the immediate outcome?

For many of us, and I was like this for years, my life was something that I passively observed. Oftentimes fearful of failure, I wouldn't put myself out there as much as I could have. I was risk-averse. Conversely, I would allow myself to be negatively affected by the fear of success. Talk about being double-minded. I couldn't win inside my own brain.

What about you? If we boiled the nuance of your life into two terms of phrase, which would you more identify with?

Is life happening to me or

am I happening to life?

Maybe these two questions would help.

Do I possess a sense of control over the things I can control?

or

Do I feel like things are consistently happening to me and all I am doing is reacting to all of these things of which I possess little to no control?

Have you ever felt like in you are not where you want to be in life, but don't know why?

Once you have determined where you are in relation to the four main spheres discussed in this book, seek wise counsel about which sphere you should focus on first.

Don't worry about whether pursuing one sphere before another is the right or wrong choice. Seek advice from some people who know you well and get their input. Pray and meditate on what your next step might be. Here are some case studies to guide you. Names have been changed to protect the innocent. :D

Callie was stuck, unsure of what their next career or church move was supposed to be. Admittedly, they discovered they were just going through the motions of life. When it came to faith, nothing seemed to energize them. Relationships with their children were healthy, but something seemed off. They lacked motivation at work because it was all the same. They had some friendships, but they weren't really going anywhere. Over the course of a couple months, Callie and I discussed the theory of where they were in relation to each of the four main spheres. We talked through how they best connect with God and they determined, they weren't sure. All they did was made sure to read the Bible, go to church, be involved in a Bible Study/Small Group, and serve on a team.

I had them read through the Spiritual Personalities profile and they determined helping others was something they enjoyed doing. So, I issued a challenge for them to look for opportunities to bless somebody. Sure enough, it wasn't difficult to identify a need and meet it. Within two weeks, they reported back speaking to three different situations that presented themselves and how they responded. Life was becoming exciting for them. Their prayer life shifted as they sought out the heart of God in their serving of others.

Another aspect of this pursuit was Callie's heart for assisting single mothers. Experiences in their life directly influenced this special awareness for single mothers. As we discussed what it would like to take a step toward this group of people, Callie found it wasn't as specific as single mothers, but other women in general. Funny enough, as they became open to looking for ways to bless other women, Callie ended up discovering and intentionally meet-

ing with three different young women as a way to do a mentoring type of relationship with them.

* * *

Jerry is in their 20's. They came to me seeking counsel on some spiritual matters. At the time of our initial meetings, Jerry was a business owner taking college courses for Bible training and vocational ministry. We talked through what the purpose of their life was supposed to be. They enjoyed the business and the people they interacted with on a daily basis, but something was tugging at them to pursue vocational ministry. At this point, Jerry had already taken some personality assessments to discover some of their natural unconscious responses to things. We also discussed how they best connected with God, since Jerry was studying the Bible and seeking vocational ministry. Jerry knew that reading and talking about spiritual things with other people helped them feel closer to God.

Jerry had a decent support network of people, but identifying a lack in some key areas within that network and their own doubts surrounding their purpose, Jerry sought me out to bridge that gap. As we talked, I asked them questions within the mindset of where Jerry was in relation to these four spheres. When it came to their purpose, Jerry really wanted to be in ministry. They enjoy working with Junior High and High School age students.

I advised them on sticking with their college courses. Additionally, their business directly impacts students and so I asked Jerry about what they were intentionally doing to bless or guide students *in the context in which Jerry works with them. Jerry said any of the moments that brings Jerry a sense of fulfillment or joy in the way Jerry really cared about happened by accident. I asked Jerry what would bring the students joy and fulfillment. Jerry replied that helping to reach certain achievements and goals in their discipline is something the students value. I told Jerry to start there. Be a champion for the achievements and goals of the students. In building that relational trust would Jerry be given more opportunities to speak into other areas of their lives.*

Sure enough, Jerry postured their heart to serve the students specific to things he was training them. This brought about a new sense of fulfillment and has only bolstered—in a good way—Jerry's desire for vocational ministry. Instead of getting bogged down by the fact Jerry's business is not a church ministry, Jerry sought to see their purpose through the lens of helping others get what they want and in so doing, it has enriched Jerry's life.

* * *

Those are just two stories. Here are some other generic examples to help guide you.

If you feel spiritually stuck, discover your preferred pathway and then seek out a study, group of people, local Pastor, etc. to assist you in determining solid next steps to become more spiritually connected to God and others.

If you feel stuck in making certain changes in your life or unsure why you do somethings certain ways and are frustrated by the lack of success in other ways, take a personality assessment. From there, entrust yourself to trusted group of people, a Life Coach, or a therapist to hold you accountable to your intentional growth of self. I highly recommend checking out the Done With Stuck Roadmap.

You cannot work on yourself by yourself.

Connecting with God and others will help in your individual growth.

Maybe you discovered you don't have as many close friends as is recommended. Think through the different places you regularly interact with certain people. Determine which of those people you think you could be friends with and then ask them to hang out! Super simple. If you are fearful of rejection, then maybe that's the first thing you work on within yourself through the help of a professional. From there, take the risk of asking to do life with people and see how they respond. If they say, "yes," then show up consistently. Don't be a clinger, learn how to communicate well, and be committed.

If you have a hard time keeping relationships, then that would be another good thing to self-assess with the help of others. How do you communicate? Seek out some relationship guide books or studies to give you the skills necessary to be an effective and endearing friend.

Purpose is tough.

If you determined your gifting and pursuing it is the next step you really want to hone in on, then maybe it's time for a Life Coach or a Life Plan. Maybe it's time to find a business partner and start that business. Pursue a college or graduate education. Maybe it's finally time to sit down and write that book. Volunteer at that shelter. Ask for that promotion. Do the project at work no one else wants to volunteer for.

Seek wise counsel.

Advocate for yourself.

The determining and the awareness part is half the battle. It's hard to know where to go if you don't know where you are, right now. Like I said before, if you take this proposal seriously, then you can head off in any number of directions and there are any number of choices for you to consider per sphere!

I cannot say this enough, seek wise counsel when it comes to your next step.

Sometimes our next steps are super simple and we just need to take one.

From here, the book will shift a bit.

Up until this point, what I set out to convey, I have done.

I invite you to continue reading the next few chapters. In them, I unpack some things to consider as you journey on.

Feel free to disembark here and endeavor to discover where you are.

The following chapters will be waiting for you, if you ever want to revisit them. If anything in this book has resonated with you, then I believe what's to follow will be most helpful.

The Process

There is no avoiding the process of life.

What technology has blessed us with in convenience has cursed us in forgetting that some things are worked out over time. Time and space has been relegated to those interested in science fiction, but in reality, time and space affects all of us. We see it in the effects of gravity on our spines and in the time aged wrinkles on our grandparents' faces.

Apparently, our hair changes color too, I have heard it called, gray, or is it grey? I refuse to acknowledge its presence on my head.

Who I am and where I am is rooted in the presence of God while the fruit of our growth is what we give the world. We can look at this using agricultural language found in the Bible. There is a lot of pictorial verbiage about trees. There are even weird verses about the Trees of Eden going down to the depths of Sheol.

People have identified with trees for centuries. Even today, a quick Google search of "tree tattoos" will give you thousands of different people showcasing the image of a tree to represent strength. This comparison is not new revelation. My hope is to look at this imagery with a different and perhaps renewed perspective.

Our advances in technology have mainly accelerated in the past 100 years. Trees have been around for eons. We'd suffocate without them. Before we commit to the following trajectory of discussing the process of discovering where I am and where to go next, I will touch on the technological process.

What we experience in an instant with our iPhone took months and years of development from a small group of people. Those people took a considerable amount of time to accomplish and bear fruit for billions of people to enjoy and utilize in instantaneous moments of use. The vast majority of us cannot relate technologically because we did not help in the process.

We only experienced the fruit of other peoples'…process.

However, most of us can relate with process through the imagery of agriculture. Especially if there are "seasonal" foods you like to enjoy. All of us started out as children, so we can on a certain level understand—in part—the maturation process of life.

From fully relying on our parents to our parents fully relying on us, we are surrounded by people at almost every stage of life. From young to old, we see the outward process of aging in people. What we do not see or maybe care to investigate are the years of their process of becoming that each of us experiences. Some of us are intentional about this process, while others don't know where to begin.

The annoying guy at work…

The embittered woman in line at the grocery store…

The person longing for a lasting monogamous relationship, but consistently move from new lover to new lover…

We see the fruits, but we neglect to consider the roots.

The thing about roots is this, the width, depth, and strength of roots are directly impacted by the quality of the soil. Like seeds, we do not get to pick where we are planted. Unlike trees, once we get to a certain age, we have the freedom to move around. However, as many are aware, not everyone possesses this freedom. More so, if we don't tend to the soil of our heart, then it matters less where we live or the people we associate with because what is happening inside means more than what is happening around us.

This is why process may be better understood through the lens of agriculture and not technology. Our brains our interesting organisms. Memory and remembering are necessary functions for effective living. The ability to take "members" of our thoughts and put them back together in the form of a memory allows for us to re-live experiences.

The odd part about re-membering—yes the hyphen is intentional—is its place in forming our who and where we are. The members of our thoughts are not just things that happened and are over, never to be revisited. We often associate memories with past experiences. I want to submit to you that these members are a collection of both past and future experiences played out in the present.

Understanding the difference in revelation (past or future), utilizing this understanding, and living it out in a manifested transformation of self is the entirety of the process.

For example, let's consider a relationship that has been betrayed. If you have not experienced something like this before, then try to think of some other situations where you have been hurt by another person.

Man meets woman. Man enjoys spending time with woman. Woman feels the same. They often enjoy each other's company. One day, man meets a different woman. Man spends time with woman and then goes to spend time with different woman. The first woman does not know this fact. One day, first woman learns of how much time man is spending with different woman. This hurts woman and she no longer wants to see man.

Time passes and woman meets new man. Woman and new man enjoy each other's company. Woman is hesitant to spend more time with new man because she fears new man may end up being like the previous man. Woman stops seeing new man.

Woman is alone. Woman wonders if she is acceptable enough for any man. Woman wonders if she is acceptable to any person. Woman wonders if she is acceptable to God.

Disclaimer, this is just an example and not some absolute truth about relationships. The woman re-membered past hurt along with future possibilities and it negatively impacted her present identity.

Sometimes it is that easy. Seems almost too simple. There is a lot to unpack in a situation described above, but the idea is this, the way we arrange the members of our thoughts impacts the outlook of our lives.

Learning how to do this in a healthy and effective way takes time. It requires process. Some things need to happen in a certain order.

What other examples can you think of?

* * *

"In process, we have to remember there is a process...."
-Banning Liebscher

We are relational beings. Things have to work in harmony with one another to really become who we were created to be. Your past experiences have either positively or negatively influenced the quality of your soil. The quality of your soil will dictate the ability for roots to grow. The quality of your root system—what is grounding you—will determine how you will grow above the surface. It will also determine how you stand up during inclement weathered seasons.

Did you know there are scientists working to create a computer that can compute faster than a human?

The internal processes of recall in our brain is faster than the fastest quantum computer. Yup, we do not have to worry about machines taking over the world—yet. Artificial intelligence is, quick. I am not saying it is slow, but compared to our brains, we win. It's not human level quick.

You may wonder, why?

Various reasons really, but one of the top reasons is that a computer has to process information and crosscheck it with other information in its system. They still haven't figured out a way to keep a computer from sorting through irrelevant data.

It can be argued that computers are faster than humans because they sort through more information and are quicker than us. Our brains can associate information quicker than a computer by sorting out the irrelevant material. Some of the brightest thinkers train their mind by creating neural pathways free of irrelevant material. We all do it. Whenever we learn new skills and go on to master a skill, we create neural pathways free from irrelevant information. In time, this speeds up and improves the quality of the process.

Unfortunately, we have gotten so used to processes being quick that we get impatient when our technology or our ability to master concepts or understand experiences requires extra time.

Discovering where you are in relation to God, yourself, others, and your purpose is a process.

To be clear, I don't want to over complicate the process. I want us to be encouraged whenever we read about accomplished people. What we read in moments and sentences often took years for the person who lived them. Over night success stories are often preceded by years of patient toiling, small wins, setbacks, and plenty of perseverance.

Ancient people understood this more than us. They understood things took time. Ancient people would wait years for the fruit of the seeds they had sown. One tree would take up to seven years to bear fruit! They had faith the fruit would come.

I want to revisit the idea of faith because we need it throughout the process. We need to be able to identify what it is, and how what I do in my response to faith is considered my belief.

The ancient writer as recorded in the Book of Hebrews said this about faith:

Faith is the <u>reality</u> of what is hoped for, the <u>proof</u> of what is not seen.

Two big things here, "reality and proof" are underlined.

Reality is a word that comes from a Greek word with huge implications. The word is *hypostasis*. That's fun to say! Hypostasis is the underlying substance of reality, and it supports everything else.

And proof in this context means to "bring into the light."

Faith is the substance of all reality bringing to the light the unseen things.

Faith and believing go together because believing means to put flesh to whatever has our faith.

If faith is what is invisible, believing is what makes it visible.

Faith is to the spiritual what believing is to the physical.

Some things require more faith than others.

For 108 years, various Chicago Cubs fans maintained a faith that each season the team would one day win the Major League Baseball World Series. For baseball fans, this seemed like a hard thing to believe in, but the fans showed up, selling out almost every home game. The waiting happened between the years of 1908 and 2016, which is over 100 years in between being crowned the champions of the sport of baseball. Not a single Cubs fan alive in 1908 was alive in 2016 to see them win again. Many Cubs fans were born and died between 1908 and 2016, they lived entire lives hoping for something that never came.

What gave them the gumption to hold onto such seemingly futile faith?

Hope?

It may not seem like it, but it requires a considerable amount of faith for two people to get married. They enter into a relationship where they believe the other person will remain faithful to the intended monogamy of their covenant.

Faith is a requirement for many things, including the theory of evolution or a random cosmic accident as an explanation for the question, "How did we get here?"

So what holds your faith?

What gives you the reason to believe in anything?

I think it's a part of our humanity. Leaning into faith and embracing the reality of its necessity gives us life. Faith in something requires risk.

Risk that it isn't true.

Risk that it is true.

Do you believe you can a live beyond the parameters of your limited imagination?

Are you willing to risk humiliation, failure, and success for a fulfilling and flourishing life?

Have faith in the process.

There is no "there," there is only "here."

Where you are in the process is the reality in which you find yourself. Avoid the disappointment of not being where you think you should be, instead assess where you are in the process in order to determine where to go next.

* * *

Where is "here?"

Keep in mind that no matter where you find yourself, once you get "there" it only becomes "here." Thus, "there" is a mirage to the accomplishment of arriving.

Life as process is to accept the reality of faith as its substance.

To "arrive" is to forgo faith and adventure.

The adventure is where you are, here, now.

It's not all a sprint.

Life is rhythm.

It is work.

It is rest.

It is giving.

It is receiving.

It is filling.

It is emptying.

It is work.

It is rest.

Here,

now.

Rhythm & Rest

---•--••●••--•---

"Therefore my heart was glad, and my tongue rejoiced. Moreover, my flesh will rest in hope…" Acts 2:26

The whole of this book and many like it are built on the premise of belief. It is not so much the power of belief, but the reality of belief's influence on our existence. This is not some philosophical New Age babble, but the convergence of one's searching and the phenomenon of infinite potentiality that is "Christ Jesus in you."

What an interesting life we all can have! Especially if we endeavor to live an interesting life.

As humans, we are the epitome of our known reality. Sure, some people find other aspects of our world to be more interesting than humans, but no other compilation of known matter can think in the existential ways we think. On the surface, humans tend to be creatures of habit, but in reality, we are beings who express themselves in an infinite amount of ways.

All of creation is the balance of matter and energy. Even the paper or electronic tablet you are holding is vibrating at an extremely low frequency. They are the compositions of atomic cells moving at a slow speed. Unlike gas or liquid where the cells move quicker giving them more vaporous or fluid states of existence, solids are solid due to the close proximity of its cellular makeup.

To discover meaning, who we are, or wherever is "here," is not about acquiring a new knowledge and exploiting it for personal gain. Furthermore, it is not about acquisition at all. Life is more about recognition and realization.

You may ask, why?

Or, what?

If God is the Creator of life. Then we can believe He gave us His breath, He gave us Himself in the form of Jesus, and He gave us His glory.

In the beginning, there was nothing to acquire, and God went to work speaking Himself into our reality and sustaining it. God is energy. God is a lot of things, more than what we can describe, and not limited to any singular "God is…" statement. This God of an infinite make up spoke matter into being, giving it energy, giving it life. It's tempting to get caught up on the vernacular or talking points of one philosophy or religion. Even with this book, the goal is the search for truth and how it pertains to the navigation of our individual and collective lives.

If God is really our energy, then He is our strength.

He gives meaning to our life.

This is recognition and realization.

* * *

Why is recognition and realization important?

For the sake of the world, of course.

Remember the mandate in the first chapter of the ancient poem? After God created man in His own image, He blessed them and said, "Be fruitful, multiply, fill the earth, subdue it, rule over it."

Do you believe this to be happening today?

Do you believe this to be true about your own life?

What are you doing about it?

What energy are you expelling to fulfill your creative purpose?

How hard are you working?

Enter the "rest."

* * *

What is this rest?

It all began within the ancient poem about Creation.

Before God told humanity to do anything, two things happened.

He created us.

He blessed us.

We get the first thing because I wrote this book, and you are reading it, which makes our existence so real.

The second thing is the prophetic key to interpreting the Bible and understanding the reality of who we are, where we are, and the next steps of our creative purpose.

The word used for "bless" in Genesis 1:28 is "Barak."

Obviously, the first thing that popped into your mind was the 48th president of the United States of America.

Some of you may have even quoted a line from Andy Mineo, "'Pac did more for me than Barack. Salute!" Different word, though.

Barak can mean, "praise."

As in, "Give Barak to the Lord, for He is good."

God created us, praised us, and in the same way we are expected to praise Him.

How cool is that?

He.

Praised.

Us.

He called us good!

Sure, we messed it up, but in this worldview, Jesus reorients us to our original design. He revealed God will stop at nothing to show each person He loves them. Just because we forgot our origin does not mean we have lost the opportunity to enter through Jesus and rest in the praise of God.

God spoke prophetically over us when He blessed us, and He was enamored by us. This was not by our doing, but by God's doing. One ancient writer said this, "and yet God's works have been finished since the foundation of the world."

God knew there was a possibility we would neglect our origin and try a different path. This is why Jesus came. To show us exactly who is God and reveal our true selves!

Jesus came to save the world, not to condemn it.

For God so loved the world, he sent Jesus.

He created the world and blessed it by creating us.

After blessing us, God commissioned us!

Our creation and our praise is God's heart revealed through Jesus. God chose to co-labor with a created version of Himself. Like the heroes of faith, if we think about where we came from, we would have an opportunity to return. We came from God, revealed through Jesus, and energized by God's Holy Spirit.

Paul told the Philippians that it was God working in them to fulfill God's purposes and desires for humanity.

The word for God working in us to live a fulfilling and flourishing life is the same Greek word! It is the word "energo." The same word we translate into English for "energy."

The word "energo" used in Phil. 2:13 is the same word used in Ephesians 6:12 when referring to the invisible forces waging war against: our minds, how we love, honor, and serve one another.

It is God as energy that created matter and it is by His energy we are transformed and sustained. There is nothing you can do to make His energy more active in your life. It is already holding the universe together! It's pretty active!

You can enter His rest, if you really want to.

The entirety of the four spheres described in this book need to be harmonized by partnering with God, resting in Him, as He does the work to make all things right in the world. Rest is something freely given. The question is on whether or not we want to realize and recognize this life transforming truth.

"But seek His kingdom, and these things. Will be provided for you. Don't be afraid, little flock, because Your Father delights to give you the kingdom." Luke 12:31-32

You see that?

This verse helps us to interpret the third part of the mandate written about in the ancient poem.

We are His creation.

We are praised by God.

So, change the world.

You cannot increase God's favor in your life in the same way you cannot decrease it. God loves you and His love for you never changes. There is nothing we can do to increase this love and there is nothing we can do to decrease it. His intentions toward us are never changing. Our realization, recognition, and receiving of this favor and love is the hurdle.

We can fail to realize, recognize, and receive the gift.

Be transformed by the renewing of your mind.

Do you believe?

Do you believe God is in you?

He is energizing you.

You are more powerful than that pink bunny with a drum.

And it all starts with where you come from.

You are loved.

You are blessed.

And it is all because of the Father who created you.

He created you because He believes in joy.

Let your mind be renewed, "So that you may discern (or test) what is the good, pleasing, and perfect (complete, without blemish, full, un-shortened) will (process of conception, divine delight becomes will along with passion) of God." Romans 12:2 The Mirror Paraphrase

The philosopher Aristotle lived before the revelation of Jesus and he said this of perfection, "Perfect is that beyond which there is no further advance in excellence or quality in its genus, which lacks nothing of its own excellence."

We don't have to attempt to be perfect people. We can rest in Christ's perfection at work in us.

It's possible the New Testament writer Paul, who wrote that verse in Romans, would have had an understanding of Aristotle's explanation of "perfect."

This is conjecture, but I imagine Paul would have had Isaiah 55:11 in mind too, "It is the same with my word. I send it out, and it always produces fruit. It will accomplish all I want it to, and it will prosper everywhere I send it."

This is the beautiful part of "resting" in the finished work of God. What He spoke into us at our creation will accomplish all He wants us to become—in the end.

Remember, God is more faithful than we are. He sent Jesus as part of that process to ensure our fulfillment, wherever we go.

Return to *where you are*.

Here.

Now.

It is our creative origin and purpose to fulfill the mandate laid out in Genesis One.

"This is what the Lord says: Stand by the roadways and look. Ask about the ancient paths: Which is the way to what is good? Then take it and find rest for yourselves..." Jeremiah 6:16

* * *

Do you believe it, yet?

Naturally, you may be thinking, "Let's say I believe it, but I don't feel it."

If this is how you feel, "How do I grow in this stuff?" Whether or not you have read the Bible, go or don't go to church, etc. it's ok. We are about discovering where we are and what our next step should be.

I get it.

The ancient teacher Jesus said; "My yoke is easy, the burden light." Sometimes, following after Jesus can feel heavy and burdensome. What I have learned is this; our perspective on this life drastically affects our understanding. There's a story in the Gospel writings about a guy named Peter. You may have heard of him. One time, he fell-with-style when attempting to walk on water.

He walked on water, until he didn't. Once he took his focus off of Jesus, he sank.

In order to do the impossible, our eyes have to stay on Jesus.

See, I graduated from a Christian college with a degree in Spiritual Formation.

I defined the program as "Helping people become the best version of themselves." I should have copyrighted that phrase because I recently heard a company using it, but I dropped the ball there.

When I graduated, I was probably at an all-time low as far as my faith was concerned.

I felt like a failure. Seriously. I had the audacity to think, "If I cannot spiritually form myself, how can I spiritually form other people?"

There is so much wrong with that question, I won't even begin to break it down. I am sure you get the point and through that lens you could understand my internal struggle and desire to tell God, "I know you're real and I get that you love me, but you're too hard. If it is this much work to be "holy," then I need a break. I know my salvation is secure and heaven sounds wonderful, but I am not going to try the route of a super-saint-Christian-guy. It isn't worth it."

I didn't get what it meant to rest in God.

I didn't get my creative origin.

I didn't know my creative purpose.

I didn't think those terms through.

I was still thinking in terms of right and wrong, a "sinner saved by grace."

I didn't come face-to-face with my orphan mentality until a couple of years after college.

Jesus in us is God in us, so it is physically impossible for us to live a fulfilling, flourishing, and beyond our imagination life without Jesus. Just to cover our bases, the Holy Spirit in us is God in us. It is God in us that gives us the energy to live the Jesus way.

When I was a kid, I was given the choice to take piano lessons or play recreational league baseball. My mother could only afford one. I was interested in piano, but I couldn't do both.

At the time I was asked to make a choice, I had been playing baseball for six years compared to the zero amount of time I spent learning the piano. Naturally, I chose baseball. It would have been hard for me to learn piano knowing I was giving up baseball. I wouldn't have had the energy for it. I wouldn't have worked towards it.

Practice?

Come on now.

That wasn't going to happen.

However, when it came to baseball.

I worked.

I played everyday, watched how others did things, and asked questions.

I worked some more.

I went to practices with a cheerful attitude, looked forward to game days, and watched Baseball Tonight, everyday.

I consistently worked.

I did not grow tired of playing baseball. I would play at recess and after school. We would play fast pitch, medium pitch, and stick ball.

#Work

I dreamt of baseball. I wore clothing with Cubs insignias on them. I loved baseball. I still do.

When it came to baseball, none of it felt like work.

I was energized.

Have you ever felt that way about something? The activity requires effort, but it gives you energy to do it.

This is the energy that puts you at rest. This is the rest of God.

When it comes to where you are and your next step, it has to come from God or we are living short of real change and transformation. This is grace. Grace is the manifestation of the power of God.

God in us is our true self, and we are here, in Him.

When we know we are loved by God—not in the "Yeah, the Bible says God loves me" kind of way —but in the "God told me He loves me" kind of way, we become energized and empowered knowing that it is a great thing to be loved by God. To know that God knows you.

Love is knowing someone by first hand experience, not simply knowing about them.

Do you feel known by God?

This is the ultimate spiritual discipline.

You can read your Bible, get up at 5 AM to pray, worship in your car, closet, and with the church, serve the poor, sport a Jesus fish sticker on your bumper, memorize the Bible, start a ministry, become an elder, volunteer in the nursery, lead a small group, and still do all of that out of a place of powerless individual effort.

We don't grow up in God by our effort, but by His effort.

Approach the disciplines in this way. Let the Holy Spirit guide you into all revelation and truth. Know your origin and it will energize you to be the version of who you were created to be.

This is what it means to be a disciple of Jesus (one who follows after the way of Jesus).

In the first century, to become a disciple of a Rabbi like Jesus meant to leave behind our livelihood and sometimes, your family. The goal in the religious community 2,000 years ago was to become a leader in the temple. To follow a teacher like Jesus, means to literally go where He goes, listen to His teachings, and do what He said to do, etc.

Your life fully encompassed your teacher's life. In time, you would become a teacher and would follow in the steps of the one who taught you. Someday, maybe you could even have your own disciples.

Some of you hear that and think, "Nah, I wouldn't want anyone following me around all the time."

Parents with young kids get this. Some of you escape to the bathroom for a moment of peace and solitude. How about pet owners? We own an Australian Shepherd and she follows us around almost all the time. If both me and my wife are at home, she goes back and forth between whom she's been following.

Could you imagine being a celebrity with the paparazzi following you around everywhere? I have watched multiple videos of people like Justin Bieber kindly confronting people following him around all day, asking them: "Hey, I know you all have a job to do, but can you for the next hour, let me have some time to myself while I go to a store?"

Discipleship in ancient times involved a consistent and close proximity.

I want to highlight something from the Gospel of John. Let's pick it up with something Jesus was recorded as saying in John 5:18-20...

"This is why the Jews began trying all the more to kill Him: Not only was He breaking the Sabbath, but He was even calling God His own Father, and making Himself equal with God.

"Then Jesus replied, "I assure you: The Son is not able to do anything on His own, but only what He sees the Father doing. For whatever the Father does, the Son also does these things in the same way. For the Father loves the Son and shows Him everything He is doing, and He will show Him greater works than these so that you will be amazed."

You hear that? The son only did what the Father does.

This is obedience.

At the core of discipleship is obedience.

Obedience can be defined as "a courageous interdependence moving into action."

This is one of the many beautiful aspects to God. He is unrelenting in His desire to work with us for the sake of others.

Following the stories in the Bible, it shows that God is choosing to work with humankind to see the coming about of the Kingdom of Heaven on Earth.

To be a disciple of Jesus is to directly partner with God in this endeavor.

We are living in the 21st Century and not the 1st Century, so what does it mean for us, today, to be a disciple of Jesus?

To answer that question, I want to tell you about the game of golf and how I found something true about discipleship from an unlikely person.

On the surface, golf isn't a difficult concept. A ball sits on the ground, you pick a golf club, you step up to the ball, and no one is going to mess with you or even talk while you swing, then boom! There it goes.

The goal of golf?

Hit the ball towards a 4.25 inch hole in the ground and get it in with as few hits of the ball as possible.

One way of comparing life to the game of golf is this, "If life is the game, the goal is to screw up as few times as possible."

And like life, as I will point out here regarding discipleship is this truth: Golf really isn't about the other players. Every player is going to score what they score. Every person in life is going to achieve or accomplish whatever, when it comes to it, here is the axiom of golf, life, and discipleship:

It's you against the course.

Our faith journeys aren't meant to be competitive. Unfortunately, comparison and association naturally happen. This comparison and association can stimulate growth, but often in the long term, it stunts it.

Each of us responds differently to Jesus.

The journey of discipleship is one of purpose-based choices, and a different level of intentionality.

Like Jesus, he endeavored Himself to do what He saw the Father doing. That was one Jesus' goals.

What about us? What are some goals you can set in your discipleship journey?

* * *

For us, I want to lean on something called Goal-setting theory. In it, the creators of this theory identified two main types of goals. They are called;

Superordinate and Subordinate

This is important, because based on how we arrive at where we are and what our next steps will be, could use a healthy tension of these $10 words: superordinate and subordinate goals.

A superordinate goal is vague or abstract. It is more akin to a theme or an anthem. It's wide open and not very specific.

For example, a superordinate goal is, "I want to be healthy."

A subordinate goal is different, they are challenging, specific, and concrete kinds of goals.

A subordinate example of healthy living would be to eat, "I will lower my sodium and fat intake by eating no bacon for 30 days."

Discipleship is a healthy entanglement of the two.

It's one thing to say, "I want to serve those less financially fortunate than me."

And another to say, "I will serve people in those situations every Tuesday at the Salvation Army for the next six weeks."

However, discipleship isn't meant to be religious. This life is about being in right relationship with God. Just like in your relationships with people, if the aspects of your relationship becomes a set of boxes to check off as you move on with your time, then you're beginning to venture into religious obligation rather than honorable relating.

You tracking with me here? Good, there's more.

I mentioned earlier about an unfortunate phenomenon within our faith journeys. About how easy it is to compare ourselves with others based on where they are in their faith journeys.

Unconsciously, we can do this with someone's testimony. There are some people with crazy awesome stories of being unlikely disciples of Jesus. One of my favorite stories is about Brian 'Head' Welch from the rock band Korn. You may have heard his story, if you haven't I want to encourage you to check it out.

He's not someone you would have—at least on the surface—suspected to discover Jesus and actively pursue Him with everything.

Unfortunately, we hear stories like his and compare it to our story and accidentally disqualify ourselves from being considered "real disciples."

We need to remember, it's us against the course. And the Holy Spirit is our caddy.

The call of being discipled by Jesus can feel strange to us.

I can tell you my perceived successes in vocational ministry, family, friends, etc and the responsibilities I am honored to steward are in many ways a result of my discipleship journey.

Being obedient and following the ways of Jesus has in many ways led me to where I am in this moment and for you to read what I have to share.

There's a lot of unlikeliness to me being here at this season of my life.

I attribute that to the grace and mercy of God. I can tell you, I didn't write this book because I have hit every shot perfectly in the golf game of discipleship.

If we are to be disciples, discovering where we are is necessary. To be a disciple of Jesus is to be seen by Him, known by Him, feel a sense of belonging in Him, and ultimately be loved by Him.

In the process of being discipled by Jesus, He will ask us to put flesh on the words we read in the Bible.

Serve one another.

Honor each other.

Pursue love.

Jesus is the way, the truth, and the life.

He is not the work, the taxes, and the living for the weekend.

The way of Jesus is the blueprint for our living. He is the truth because He is the exact representation of the Father's heart. He is the life because when we know by experience the truth of God and live in a way that serves and honors others, in this we find our life as well.

What God desires for us is greater than any desire we can hope to have for ourselves. When our desire and His wisdom-filled desire align, that's when life becomes next-level adventurous for us.

To follow Jesus as a disciple today is to live like Jesus in whatever context we currently find ourselves.

There's a connection of all things. Our relationship with God, ourselves, others, and creation are entangled in our heart of service. We cannot discover where we are apart from whom we serve.

We serve God as the Creator of our identity.

We serve ourselves best in how we serve others.

We serve creation because it is where we live.

There's a story in the Gospels of an ordinary man afflicted by an extraordinary spirit of "many." He encountered Jesus, was saved, healed, and delivered from the curse of the "many." Which got me thinking about us in the 21st Century and the many ordinary things that distract us from knowing where we are and where we are going.

After encountering Jesus, the man was given a focused directive on what to do next.

What if we can experience a form of that, today?

If we are encumbered by "many" whatever that "many" means; problems, successes, finances, lack of finances, things, coverings or coping mechanisms, etc. then we shouldn't be surprised whenever we find ourselves not following Jesus the way we should.

* * *

Back in 2012, I lived in Phoenix, AZ working at a university four days a week and playing golf six days a week. I had a subordinate goal of becoming a pro golfer within three years. I was also finishing up my master's degree. I had many things going on.

One of the first things I did in pursuing a golfing career was find a coach. Someone who could work with me 1:1 and help me become as much of a golfer as I could be.

When we started, he told me that he was going to dismantle everything I knew about my golf swing. In so doing, he would have me do singular awkward movements hundreds of times.

He told me that in golf, as much as in life, perception is our reality, and in golf what we think we are doing is different from what is actually happening.

He said a golf swing isn't built on any particular thing, but it is the synchronization of these seemingly individual and counterintuitive movements that makes all the difference.

So I trained, and one move after the other, he coached me through putting my swing back together piece by piece, one step at a time.

It was arduous.

One day while training, I sensed the voice of the Father saying, "What Larry is teaching you about golf is what I am going to do with your life."

One thing at a time.

One discipline at a time.

One season at a time.

One person at a time.

One risk at a time.

This has stuck with me for the past decade.

I have noticed and began to ask questions like these,

"God, what is the one thing you are trying to teach me in this season?"

"Who is the one person you have put in my life to disciple for this season?"

"What is that one thing I can do for my wife this week to help her feel seen, known, and loved by me?"

Often times, the way to where we are, begins with questions of how we are serving God, others, and Creation.

Have you watched the movie, *Tangled*? Spoiler alert ahead.

Here's the gist: A king and queen gave birth to a princess. As an infant, the princess got kidnapped by a witch. The witch kept the princess locked up in a tower and raised her as her own child. The princess grew up not knowing she was a princess.

She drew pictures and painted scenes from what she thought were her imagination. As she grew older, she desired more and more to leave the tower and explore the world. She did not know she was a captive of that tower. Unexpectedly, a young man found her and broke her out of her captivity. They went on an adventure that ended with her returning to her original home, the palace. There she learned of her real origin and parents.

She grew up with a sense of another life, but chalked it up to her imagination.

Was she still a princess even though she wasn't living like a princess?

Did her lifestyle undermine her real identity?

Tangled is one of my favorite "identity" movies out there. Coincidentally, the actor and actress who lent their voices to the main characters are both followers of Jesus.

People who believe in their creative origin.

The princess is you and me.

Born of royalty, taken captive by many distractions, set free by a young man who accompanies us on our journey to discover the king is our father.

Whoa.

The imperative from this story is knowing you have access to the palace. Too many followers of Jesus believe in the stories of their imaginative origin, but are too afraid to leave their tower of captivity and find the palace in which they were born!

Jesus came to point us to the Father, Our Creator.

Jesus said, "I am the door."

The access is here, now.

There is a rhythm & a rest to it.

Rest in the reality of Jesus.

Parting Thoughts:

You have my permission to be sad our journey is over and simultaneously happy we went all this way together! Really, your adventure is about to begin. Hopefully, in what you read, the assessments you took, the conversations you had, you discovered some renewed insight and inspiration. Here is the invitation, it's up to you and me to pursue an intentional life like you've never before lived.

I recommended the resources to pursue. Upon intentionally assessing these four areas, partner with the Holy Spirit to determine what is the next step you are to take in this faith journey of yours.

Hopefully, in this, you might identify with the younger son from the ancient parable at the beginning of this book. If you are at your wits end, wondering, "How did I get here…"

Then I hope the conversations expressed in this book and your engagement with it will move you to "go home." Return to the harmony of connecting with God, yourself, others, and your purpose.

If where you are is not "home," then it is time to discover where you are. Hopefully this book helps you get to where is your "here."

And from here, you know where to go.

If we all discover or (re)discover our right relationship to our Creator, ourselves, others, and Creation; I have faith we will all be better off.

Have a question or want to say "Hello!" connect with me at:

nolanrecker.com

Facebook

Instagram

Twitter

& TikTok

Footnotes:

[1] Smithstein, Samantha. Psy.D., "Where Are You?" https://www.psychologytoday.com/us/blog/what-the-wild-things-are/201503/where-are-you

[2] Prepared by Keas Keasler (Friends University) Material adapted from Gary Thomas', Sacred Pathways

www.ingramcontent.com/pod-product-compliance
Lightning Source LLC
Chambersburg PA
CBHW022015290426
44109CB00015B/1182